I0458791

31 Days to Emergency Preparedness and Personal Resilience

Colonel Robert Fagan, CEM

U.S. Army (Ret.)

Copyright © 2025
by Robert Fagan

All Rights Reserved.

No part of this publication may be reproduced, stored in a retrieval system, or transmitted in any form or by any means—electronic, mechanical, photocopying, recording, or otherwise—without the prior written permission of the author.

Published by Robert Fagan

Printed in the United States of America

First Edition: 2025

Dedication

To my family,

You are the reason it all matters.

To my children, Sofia and Dario, whose curiosity and willingness to learn about preparedness as children inspired hope that these lessons will carry forward into their adult lives.

And to my beloved wife, Magaly, your unwavering love, patience, and support have been the foundation of every endeavor, every mission, and every step of this journey for more than thirty years. This book, like so much about my work, is possible because of you.

~Robert

Acknowledgments

The knowledge, experience, and resilience contained within these pages are not mine alone. They are the collective wisdom of the countless men and women I have had the privilege to serve alongside throughout my career. From dozens of militaries across the globe to dedicated humanitarian workers, firefighters, law enforcement officers, search and rescue teams, emergency medical personnel, and public health officials, each has shared lessons forged in adversity and strengthened by service.

To every responder, planner, and quiet professional who gave freely of their experience, you have left an indelible mark on me. Your courage in the face of disaster, your selfless commitment to others, and your unshakable resilience are reflected in these words. While the names are far too numerous to mention, know that I carry your examples with me on every page of this work.

Enthusiastically, I affirm that all your knowledge passed on to me has made this book possible. It demonstrates a fundamental pillar of wisdom: all humanitarian action, all emergency management, and all business continuity planning ultimately begin with the most essential step—individual emergency preparedness.

About the Author

Robert J. Fagan is an experienced international emergency management executive, global humanitarian consultant, and dynamic keynote speaker with over 25 years of leadership in emergency preparedness, international disaster response, and national security. During his military career, he deployed to conflict zones, volunteered for peacekeeping and peace enforcement duties, served in combat search and rescue, and worked on multiple humanitarian assistance and disaster response projects responding to tropical storms, landslides, earthquakes, flooding, and hurricanes. A retired U.S. Army Colonel and Certified Emergency Manager (CEM), he has trained thousands in crisis leadership, emergency planning, public health response, and organizational resilience across more than 100 countries. His distinguished career includes service with the U.S. Small Business Administration, U.S. Department of State, Office of the Secretary of Defense, U.S. Army Staff, NATO Staff, and multiple U.S. embassies, where he led complex all-hazards planning, evacuations, and emergency management exercise programs.

Robert is a graduate of the U.S. Army and Air Force War Colleges, the Brazilian Army Command and Staff College, and holds graduate degrees in National Security Studies, International Relations, Strategic Intelligence, and Global Management. He is also a graduate of premier crisis leadership executive programs at Harvard, Yale, the London School of Economics, and the NATO Crisis Management and Disaster Response Centre of Excellence. With the U.S. Federal Emergency Management Agency (FEMA), he has graduated from their Master Exercise Practitioner Program and National Emergency Management Advanced and Executive Academies.

As the author of "31 Days to Emergency Preparedness and Personal Resilience," Robert empowers individuals, families, and organizations to act before disaster strikes. Through executive coaching, business continuity consulting, and engaging public speaking, he inspires audiences to view preparedness not as fear-based but as a journey of hope, confidence, and care for those we love.

Table of Contents

Introduction

Why You Need This Book

I found my life's direction at the age of six. Growing up, our family would try to take a vacation once a year. Usually, we went to Florida, which provided a much-needed break from the Midwestern winter weather. I loved these vacations because I could go on long walks with my mother at the beach or somewhere else with no destination in mind. When I was six years old, we walked to a park in Islamorada, Florida, that had an unassuming granite memorial, and the plaque read:

"This memorial is in memory of the war veterans and the civilians whose lives were tragically lost in the hurricane of September 2nd, 1935."

The memorial has a certain beauty to it that's hard to explain.

I remember the wind-blown palm trees caught my attention because I wasn't used to seeing them in that position, and I didn't understand what caused that reaction. I asked my mother, and she said that a strong hurricane had come through the Florida Keys and killed hundreds of people. I was stunned. It was a sunny day, but how could this have happened?

"Weather changes," my mother said gently, "and we do not have these storms where we live," she further explained.

I was still struck by this. "Will there be a hurricane today?" I asked.

"No," she laughed, "The weather is nice today and you don't need to worry about it."

I was still worried about it, and my concern was enough to make me want to know more of this story. I kept bothering my mother to find someone who could tell us more. We went into a local bookstore, and the person working there happened to know a lot more about the local history than we expected. She related that the hurricane started as a very weak tropical storm around the Bahamas, but by the time it moved westward, it had grown stronger and stronger until it began reaching full hurricane status. By the next day, when it arrived at the Florida Keys (a chain of islands off the southern coast of Florida), it had arrived at its full deadly potential as a Category five hurricane. For the next two days, it ravaged the coast of west Florida. By this time, authorities started counting the loss of life; over 400 people perished due to both the winds and the storm surge, which reached a peak of nearly 20 feet. The problem was that although people knew that a storm was on its way, there was very little transport infrastructure to cope with a large-scale evacuation. The main transport links bringing cargo to the Keys from mainland Florida were restricted to one railroad line. Those owning the railroad did not consider using the line for an emergency escape route. The upper or nearer mainland portion of the railroad sent a train consisting of ten empty train cars down to get people out of the area, but upon reaching Upper Matecumbe Key, it was hit by the storm surge and the winds, which knocked the train off the track. This prevented any further chance of an evacuation. To compound the tragedy, dozens of World War I-stranded veterans died working on a government-funded work program in the area.

As sad as it was to learn about these events, this tragedy served a purpose. It caused me to want to learn more. I have been interested in emergencies and disasters ever since that day—especially in terms of personal preparation and mitigation. Although we cannot prevent every emergency and disaster since we do not always know when things will happen, we can always be better prepared for life's eventualities when facing human-caused and natural disasters.

I study emergency management and crisis leadership, so you do not have to. I mean this. This book seeks to solve the problem of basic individual emergency preparedness that has been going on for decades. There is no lack of information, but people do not do it. Preparedness is a choice, and most people are underprepared for emergencies. Why do we not get better prepared? There are many reasons that I will explain later in the areas of cognitive and unconscious bias, and our own proclivities to believe in positive outcomes. Some will say time, resources, lack of information, or availability of materials all inhibit them from being better prepared. However, the number one thought running through most people's minds is *This will never happen to me*. Yet, it will.

How did we get this way? Part of the answer has to do with the professionalization of first-response organizations and advances in medical care around the world. Having law enforcement, fire, search and rescue, and emergency medical forces able to respond within ten minutes in most nations makes us outsource our safety and security to those entities. We depend on them, and we should, but we also have to take care of ourselves for those crucial first ten minutes. However, in a large-scale multi-jurisdictional disaster, nobody is coming to get you for a very long time because they are busy saving lives and stabilizing the incident.

This is why you need this book. Bad things can happen to good people at any time. Emergency preparedness is always something we are going to do tomorrow, and tomorrow just does not get here. It is the icing on life's cake. Something that makes it better and sweeter later. My philosophy to you is to start thinking of emergency preparedness as the flour of life's cake, or rather, an indispensable component. Let's get busy, quit making excuses, and finally become prepared for emergencies and increase our resilience through this 31-Day program. People and families who plan for emergencies will help keep people safe, limit property damage, know what to do before, during, and after a disaster, better manage their savings, support community preparedness, and help their community get back up and running after a disaster.

Did you know that local, state, and national governments globally think you have planned to be okay in the face of disaster? It is true. Barring the threat to life, limb, property, and the environment, most governments around the world consider citizens generally prepared for seventy-two hours or three days and use that for various emergency planning factors, such as ordered evacuations and community disaster recovery. Are you and your family prepared for basic emergencies for three days? In this program, I will walk you through how to have a readiness mindset and get yourself and those you love better prepared for almost any emergency in just 31 days. In this book, we will have one requirement or reflection per day in the form of a task called "Your Turn," where you complete the item or thought for the day. Do this one day at a time. There is no need to work ahead. As a matter of fact, I discourage it. Make this simple and achievable. Many might jump into this and start reading and doing, only to be overwhelmed by it and not return. Do not let this happen to you. If you must stop, just start again where you left off. Emergency preparedness is a marathon and not a sprint. Slow and steady wins the race. "Go slow to go fast," as the search and rescue profession often says in training. Perhaps put it on your calendar each day for an hour and be done. For those who would like a little extra, I have a "Pro Tip" on each day for an extra thought or task you may want to consider in your preparedness journey. An average person in any country can use this book for basic emergency preparation. At the end of each day, I give you more resources for your own research, interest, and deeper planning. This book will increase your survivability and help you not only survive but thrive after an emergency or disaster. This is not an extreme survival book for absolute worst-case scenarios, but it will cover over ninety percent of what humankind faces. I have done everything for you, and all you must do is follow along, learn, and take each day as a step to being better prepared over a short amount of time. Shall we get started?

Day 1
Plan to Make a Plan

If you fail to plan, you are planning to fail.

–Benjamin Franklin

Plans are nothing; planning is everything.

–Dwight D. Eisenhower

This concept is so crucial that it gets two quotes above. Very few things work without a plan, so Day 1 of our program is about planning for personal emergency preparedness and resilience. Your steady, deliberative planning and action will create emergency preparedness and personal resilience. Every step will get you closer to the goal. The key is to get started and build momentum for quick wins and success. The first thing we need to plan for is the right mindset. Attitude is EVERYTHING. Emergency preparedness is an active choice and not a passive consequence. Keep in mind the rule of three for survival. You cannot survive three minutes without air, three hours without shelter (in inhospitable conditions), three days without water, three weeks without food, and, most importantly, three SECONDS WITHOUT THE RIGHT ATTITUDE. A prepared attitude is action-oriented and informed, prioritizing self-help before assisting others. A victim's attitude is passive, uninformed, and waiting for help. Which one are you right now?

Emergency preparedness and personal resilience are a journey and never a final destination because our situations change. We move, go to school or training, change jobs, start a family, and experience changes in our family dynamics. All sorts of things change our preparedness needs, and we need to keep up through planning and having an active, action-oriented mindset towards these changes. We all woke up today with a certain level of preparedness. Perhaps we've made some progress, but our planning could still be improved. Perhaps we have not started yet. The most important thing we need to do on Day 1 is realize that everyone can be better prepared. We should not outsource our safety and security to first-response organizations that might be overwhelmed during large-scale disasters. You got this. Following the tasks and guidance for the next 31 days will increase your preparedness and resilience. This will go a long way in improving your attitude about emergency preparedness and creating momentum to do more. This can even be fun! Plan now to spend about an hour or so per day throughout the program and open your mind positively toward preparedness. We can all work on changing our attitudes towards the task of emergency preparedness and accept the fact that being prepared is our responsibility.

Your Turn: On a scale of one to ten, evaluate your own preparedness level. Where do you stand? Place this answer on the notes page of this chapter. Take the personal preparedness oath.

Personal Preparedness Oath: "I (State your name) understand that personal emergency preparedness is an individual responsibility for me and my family, no matter where I am in the world or what I am doing. I will make every effort to prepare myself with knowledge, resources, supplies, information, organization, and first aid skills to survive without government or first responder assistance for three days. (Signed)

Pro Tip: Believing nobody will come to your rescue in an emergency allows for better planning in our minds. We are not just trying to get through several minutes; remember, our respective governments think we can get through three days without assistance. Let's prove them right.

Resources for Day 1: Plan to Make a Plan

The U.S. Federal Emergency Management Agency (FEMA) website Ready.gov is the best overall planning source for everything in this book. Start with the planning section below. Most of what we will discuss during the program can be examined in more depth here.

https://www.ready.gov/plan

Another great resource for emergency planning and preparedness is the American Red Cross.

https://www.redcross.org/get-help/how-to-prepare-for-emergencies/make-a-plan.html

Notes

_____

_____

_____

_____

_____

_____

_____

_____

_____

_____

Day 2
Build a Kit or "Go" Bag

The Future Belongs to Those Who Prepare for it today.

– Malcom X

In an emergency, how quickly could you leave your home? Consider this real-life example: On the evening of February 3, 2023, a freight train derailed in East Palestine, Ohio, United States. The train was carrying hazardous materials when thirty-eight cars derailed. Several railcars burned for more than two days, and emergency crews also conducted controlled burns of several railcars, which released hydrogen chloride and phosgene into the air. As a result, residents within a 1-mile (1.6-kilometer) radius were evacuated, and many could not return for days. Initially, the entire community of approximately 4,500 residents was told to leave within ten minutes. Can you do this?

As it happens, there is a name for this type of intentional preparation when you are building an emergency kit: these kits are generally referred to as "go bags." It makes sense, right? You have a bag that holds the things you need to go. These days, though, many of the things that you would traditionally include in that physical bag can also be digitized, and we will discuss that soon on Day 5.

So, with all that in mind, we will talk about how to build your go bag.

Everyone needs a kit or go bag to evacuate--plain and simple. In an emergency, you need to be prepared with key essential items and have a plan to take them somewhere else. Therefore, today, we want to create an emergency go bag designed just for us. This should be a portable kit that includes the items you will need to survive while you are away from home. You should be able to carry and transport it easily. We will use a three-day planning factor for this matter, as we may not know our destination, accommodation, travel distance, duration of our stay, or the availability of necessary items upon arrival. Each person and family must assess their own needs in this regard. There is no one-size-fits-all go bag because the size of your family, medical needs, and gender and age-specific requirements vary. However, standard recommendations for a starter set and the most important items include the following:

1. First Aid Kit (See Day 19 for basic items in a personal first-aid kit)
2. Water (1 gallon or 2 liters per person per day)
3. Food (3 days non-perishables)
4. Medicines or prescriptions applicable to your situation
5. Can opener, eating utensils, multi-tool with a knife blade
6. Radio (hand crank and solar charged)

7. Flashlight

8. Cell phone charger

9. Batteries and power sources for items you need

10. Hand cleaner

11. Matches and other fire-starting materials

12. Whistle (use a plastic pea-less whistle for long-lasting durability)

13. Sturdy Work Gloves

14. Extra seasonal clothing

15. Warm/Dry outerwear that is waterproof, such as a rain poncho or jacket

16. Pet supplies (more about pets on Day 24)

As you assemble your go bag, consider what materials to use for carrying your items. Small day-trip backpacks work great. This will also limit you to the weight and size of items you can take. This is a good thing because most people tend to try to take too much. Try to limit yourself to twenty pounds (or 9 kg). Remember, you might be walking a long way or carrying this in minimal spaces. Err on the side of caution. Take what you need, but remember, you need what you take. Those who live in more varied environments may want to consider changing or "seasonal" go bags for summer and winter. Once everyone has a go bag, put the bags in a place where everyone can quickly get to them, such as the closet by your front door or in an easily accessible place in your garage. Do not put them in attics, under large heavy items, or stack them behind lots of things. Think like the folks of East Palestine above, in that you have ten minutes to leave.

By this time, you might be saying to yourself, "Can I just buy one of these?" Of course, you can! There are some nice ones out there. Just be aware of the weight, the actual items it contains, and check everything for usefulness as it pertains to your situation. If you buy a go bag, pull everything out, know where it is in the bag, take everything out of the shipping plastic, and add the personal items you still need.

We do not always evacuate in emergencies. The "staying where you are" version of this planning is called sheltering in place. Making a go bag helps you shelter in place by providing quick access to the essentials you need. But if told to simply stay put for the next three days in your home or apartment, are you prepared to do that? There are many instances where this could happen quickly, such as during civil unrest or, as we saw during the COVID-19 era, during "lockdowns" for pandemics or after large-scale disasters. If local authorities told you not to go to the store or pharmacy for the next three days, do you have everything on hand you will need?

Your Turn: Use the list and get started on go bags for you and every member in your home. It does not have to be perfect at first, but your own resilience and growth need to jump into this task and "do something" right now about this vexing problem. Act and get started. Do not put it off. If you have children, get them involved in creating go bags and make this a fun activity for everyone.

Pro Tip: Soldiers constantly improve their "foxhole" or trench where they are protected from the enemy. Commit to continually improving your go bag by seeking out better and lighter options, regularly assessing the serviceability of your gear, and updating items that have expired or clothes sizes that no longer fit. Nobody wants dead batteries or rotten food during an emergency.

Resources for Day 2: Build a Kit or Bag

There are lots of resources out there for building go bags. Our Canadian friends in British Columbia have a good one that is clear, concise, and in multiple languages with videos. Don't forget to check YouTube for this topic, which literally has dozens of videos.

https://www2.gov.bc.ca/gov/content/safety/emergencymanagem ent/preparedbc/build-an-emergency-kit-and-graband-go-bag

Many government entities have go bag or disaster kit guidance. Be sure to check your local and state government websites, which might have more specific information for your area. This public-facing

U.S. Department of State guidance is clear and concise, which could involve foreign travel or residing abroad.

https://www.state.gov/global-community-liaisonoffice/crisis-management/packing-a-go-bag-and-a-staybag/

Global Rescue Go Bag Guidance
https://www.globalrescue.com/common/blog/detail/travelemergency-preparation-gobag-supplies/

Sonoma County, California Office of Emergency Readiness, Response, and Recovery Go Bag Guidance with videos.

https://socoemergency.org/get-ready/build-akit/personal-go-bags/

Notes

_____

_____

_____

_____

_____

_____

_____

_____

_____

_____

Day 3
Build a Kit for Your Car

It is not always possible to be the best, but it is always possible to improve your own performance.

– Jackie Stewart

You're watching your favorite program on a winter evening and realize you forgot to get milk today, as your spouse had asked. So, lightly dressed and confidently, you get in your car with just a light jacket even though it is slightly below freezing and snowing outside. That is not a big deal because the store is just down the road, and your car warms up quickly. On the way, you are slightly distracted by something in the road, and when you swerve to miss it, you hit a patch of ice and slide off. Luckily, your car remains upright, and you slide sideways down a large embankment into a large fresh pile of snow that has collected at the bottom. You're really stuck, and your car is buried in fresh snow. Although you are physically okay for now, you've forgotten your phone. It is getting late, and although you can see the road you recently left, there is no traffic passing by at this time of night. The hill is too steep, and the snow too deep to climb. Could this happen to you? Of course, it could happen to anybody, and this is a true story. Snow does not have to be the culprit. There are dozens of things that would leave you physically fine but trapped in or near your car. We should treat our modes of transportation like survival bubbles, just as we prepared a go bag for evacuation. Having a go bag in each vehicle is essential. This is not just a task for rural, desert, or mountainous areas. Most people spend a lot of time in their vehicles. Even if you go a few miles from home, you may be stuck in snarled traffic for hours, lost, or needing to take lengthy detours. Having some key items can save your life and keep you healthy.

Keep items in your car in a waterproof pack or sturdy canvas bag so everything is together and easy to grab. Make one for each vehicle. Here are some basic things for your consideration:

1. First aid kit
2. Paper maps with evacuation routes pre-marked
3. Battery or crank radio
4. Phone charger
5. Flashlight or headlamp with extra batteries and bulbs
6. Blanket, the small emergency ones are cheap and small. Blankets aren't just for warmth. They are the first line of defense in preventing shock.
7. Water
8. Non-perishable foods

9. Extra clothes, including sturdy shoes and socks

10. Rain jacket or poncho

11. Personal hygiene items (hand sanitizer, moist towelettes, toilet paper, tissues, toothbrush and toothpaste, tampons)

12. Plastic bags that seal

13. Shovel (small collapsible)

14. Short rubber hose (for siphoning fuel)

15. Small fire extinguisher (5 lb. ABC type)

16. Basic tools such as a tire repair kit, jumper cables, screwdriver, pliers, and multi-tool

17. Work gloves

Your Turn: Just like the go bag in your home or apartment, use the car kit list and get started on one for every vehicle you and your family drive. You spend a lot more time driving than you may realize, and anything could happen. They don't have to be perfect at first, but your own resilience and growth need to jump into this task, act, and do something –not later, but right now.

Pro Tip: Consider keeping an extra phone in your car for emergency communication. You may be stuck somewhere for a long time, either on the road or in a repair shop while traveling. Additionally, everyone should practice changing a tire. Knowing how to do this will save time and effort on the side of a busy highway and keep you safer by getting stuck for a shorter amount of time.

Resources for Day 3: Build a Kit for Your Car

There is no shortage of car kits on the market. If you decide to purchase one, go ahead and spend a little extra on quality and completeness.

California Highway Patrol emergency car kit suggestions. https://www.chp.ca.gov/programs-services/servicesinformation/roadside-emergency-kit

The Allstate insurance site is very complete and discusses multiple contingencies.

https://www.allstate.com/resources/car-insurance/caremergency-kit-list

The AAA suggestions below are short and comprehensive. https://www.aaa.com/autorepair/articles/what-to-have-inyour-car-emergency-kit

Notes

_____

_____

_____

_____

_____

_____

_____

_____

_____

_____

_____

_____

_____

_____

_____

_____

_____

_____

Day 4
Build an Office Stay Bag

Life doesn't get easier or more forgiving; we get stronger and more resilient.

– Steve Maraboli

It is late in the day, and you are trying to finish a project for your boss by tomorrow. You have been working all day and have not been paying attention to the weather. When you look up, you can see that it is getting very dark outside. Suddenly, the weather alert sounds on your phone for a tornado warning. You know this means there is an actual tornado somewhere in the area. You look around and notice that other people in your office are receiving the same warning on their phones. In an overabundance of caution, those still at work go to the basement to an extensive training room with no windows and remain there. The power goes out, but the backup generator kicks on, and everyone notices there is no cellular service. This must be due to a problem with local cell phone towers. A couple of people in the group have cellular services contracted from outside the area that depend more on satellite, and they have service. After almost an hour, most of the bad weather has passed. Local officials are asking everyone to shelter in place as the damage is extensive, with downed power lines and large debris fields that block traffic in all directions. Officials urge the public to stay off the roads while first responders attend to what will be a large incident stabilization and life-saving effort. You will probably have to remain in your office for several more hours. Are you prepared to do this?

We spend a lot of time in our workplaces. Make sure you are ready for unexpected emergencies! When I talk to people who have had to do this, most were physically fine but realized they would have to "get comfortable" for the next several hours in their work clothes with nothing to eat, pass the time, or charge their phones. If you have to stay at work for an extended period, having a few preparedness items with you will make your stay less painful. You can easily place these items in a gym bag under your desk. Here is a suggested list:

1. Small first aid kit
2. Water
3. Phone charger
4. Battery or crank radio
5. Sleep system of a light sleeping bag, mat, and a small pillow
6. Flashlight or headlamp with extra batteries and bulbs
7. Blanket, the small emergency ones are cheap and small. Blankets aren't just for warmth. They are the first line of defense in treating shock
8. Water
9. Non-perishable foods

10. Rain jacket or poncho

11. Personal hygiene items (hand sanitizer, moist towelettes, toilet paper, tissues, toothbrush and toothpaste, tampons)

12. Comfortable clothes for changing, including a sweatshirt or sweater

13. A good book you've been meaning to read

14. Work gloves (protecting hands, if need be, especially from broken glass)

Your Turn: Just like the go bag in your home or apartment and the car kit for your vehicle, use the office list and get started on an office bag for your workplace. We often spend eight to twelve hours a day at work, so you need to prepare to stay longer. Your office bag doesn't have to be perfect at first, but it is crucial for your resilience and growth to act and start making progress right now.

Pro Tip: Just like in your car kit, keep a hard copy of a book you've been meaning to read to stay positive and relieve frustration and stress. You have no idea how long you will be there, and you may not have access to other forms of entertainment or ways to pass the time. Test this plan by "camping" at your office for an extra hour sometime to gauge the viability of the items you have and your plan's completeness. Can you take a shower somehow? Would you be able to sleep? Do you have access to potable water? Encourage others to have their own work bags. First, helping everyone is the right thing to do, and second, the better prepared those around you are, the less they need your stuff!

Resources for Day 4: Build an Office Kit

There is no shortage of emergency work kits for purchase. What we have learned from go bags and vehicle kits applies here, too. The link below to Lifesecure includes multiple contingencies for offices.

https://www.lifesecure.com/office-emergency-kit-checklist/

Like building a go bag, this website from the U.S. Centers for Disease Control offers considerations for individuals with disabilities or those with access and functional needs (See Day 24).

https://www.cdc.gov/disability-emergencypreparedness/people-with-disabilities/build-a-kit.html

Notes

_____

_____

_____

_____

_____

_____

_____

_____

_____

Day 5
Your Virtual or Digital Go Bag

Fall seven times, stand up eight.

– Japanese Proverb

Thus far, we have discussed the need to have some ready supplies in a go bag or kit in our living spaces, in our cars, and at work. What about our electronic lives? Our digital lives have evolved to the point where many of the essential documents of life are only in electronic form. If you had that same ten minutes to evacuate, would you be ready to do so digitally? Here is another scenario beyond evacuation: You are away from home, and you find out there was a fire. Are you confident that you have all your important information somewhere you can access? Dealing with emergencies and then recovery will occur in multiple layers. Imagine trying to call an insurance company when the lines are all tied up. When you finally get through, you need to provide them with the information they require, all while being far from home and in crisis. You may have renter's insurance, but when you're trying to account for your antique baseball card collection, which ones did you have? Many things cannot be replaced. Photos are a great example. Finding a way to organize and digitize these things means you don't have to worry about material items, allowing you to focus on safety and the people you care about. The more you can do to be prepared ahead of time, the better. That means not only having your documents in a place you can access, but also knowing what documents you need in the first place. While this type of file organization started out for me in response to moving several times, it has helped in many other ways. I always know where my files are to give to my tax preparer, and I have implemented a good backup strategy, which means I am confident my electronic life is protected and accessible.

Many of the things that you'd traditionally include in that physical go bag in file folders can also be digitized. So, with all that in mind, we will discuss how to build your virtual or digital go bag.

What Documents Do I Need in My Emergency Kit?

Just because you can digitize something, it does not mean that it should be your only copy. There are some things that you just flat-out need to have in person, like your driver's license and passport, though some locations around the world have experimented with digital wallets that contain official, legal copies of those things. Nevertheless, having a digital backup of your important physical documents means that you will have the information to replace them, if needed.

After that, you can break your virtual or digital go bag checklist into a few different categories:

- Household Identification

- Financial and Legal Information • Medical Information

- Emergency Contact Information

- Valuables and Priceless Personal Items

I like to use information from the U.S. Federal Emergency Management Agency (FEMA) list of essentials, and I have added a few notes as well. We will consider each category individually.

Household Identification

These are the things you need to prove you are who you say you are, and to prove that your kids, pets, and spouse are, in fact, your kids, pets, and spouse. This is important when traveling or going to a temporary shelter. Although it may not seem essential, there are entire organizations dedicated to reuniting families and pets after emergencies, a task that is not easy. Imagine being divorced and without custody papers in an emergency. Sure, courts have records of those agreements, but sometimes those papers take weeks or months to obtain.

Vital Records: Birth certificates, marriage agreements, divorce decrees, adoption or custody papers.

Identity Records: Passports, driver's license, other identification cards such as employment or military, Social Security card, green card, visas, and military service records.

Pet Records: Pet ownership papers, identification tags, vaccination records, microchip information.

Financial and Legal Information

If your home or income is affected during a disaster, you'll need documentation to request assistance from your insurance company or government disaster assistance programs. This includes businesses. Remember that even after you get assistance, there are tax implications down the road. Both of those processes take time, so in addition to having your information organized and ready to go, try to keep some emergency cash on hand during high-risk periods (See Financial First Aid in Day 20).

- **Housing Documents:** Lease or rental agreements, mortgage agreement, home equity line of credit, house or property deed, and lists of/receipts for repairs.
- **Bills:** Utility bills, student loans, alimony, child support, elder care, gym memberships, streaming services.
- **Vehicle Documents:** Loan documents, VIN number, registration, title.

- **Financial Accounts:** Checking, savings, debit cards, credit cards, retirement accounts, investment accounts.
- **Insurance Policies:** Homeowners, renters, auto, life, flood, fire.
- **Note:** Don't forget to document your property! Make a list of items covered by insurance, including their estimated values, and take pictures of everything of value.
- **Sources of Income:** Pay stubs, government benefits, alimony, child support, rent payments, 1099 income.
- **Tax Statements:** Federal/state income tax returns, property tax, vehicle tax.
- **Estate Planning:** Wills, trusts, powers of attorney.

Medical Information

Even more so than the other sections on this list, it is important to make sure you have thorough documentation for each member of your household. Remember that there are some items on this list that you will need sooner rather than later, like prescription refills. Make sure that allergy information is front and center, especially life-threatening allergies (like to seafood or nuts)

- **Insurance Information:** Health and dental insurance, Medicare, Medicaid, Veterans Administration (VA) health benefits.
- **Medical Records:** List of medications, illnesses/disabilities, immunizations, allergies, prescriptions, medical equipment and devices, pharmacy information.
- **Legal Documents:** Living will, medical powers of attorney, Do Not Resuscitate (DNR) documents, caregiver agency

contracts, disabilities documentation, and Social Security benefits information.

- **Contact Information:** A list of doctors, specialists, dentists, and pediatricians.

(Emergency) Contact Info

Finally, you'll want all the contact information you may need in one place—it will save you time and headaches when you're trying to make calls, plus you may be able to delegate some phone calls to others. The exercise is useful for recalling miscellaneous items you may have forgotten in other documents and will also aid you in your family communication plan, which is scheduled for Day 6.

Bonus: You can keep a list of extensions or direct phone lines and skip the automated phone tree. Consider having the following:

- Employers
- Schools
- Houses of worship
- Homeowners' associations
- Home repair services
- Relatives/emergency contacts
- Utility companies
- Insurance companies
- Lawyers
- Local non-emergency services
- Government agencies

Valuables and Priceless Personal Items

Most of the things that fit in this section probably won't be digitized—your wedding dress, military medals, jewelry, and the like. Still, don't forget that those things may have a paper trail you want to keep in your records, especially if you have additional insurance on things like jewelry and collectibles. Consider photos here, too. While most of us now use our smartphones as cameras, this implies storing pictures somewhere other than the phone and backing up our mobile device. Don't forget to digitize all of your photos, including the ones passed down by relatives, taken by professionals, and so on.

Digital Go Bag Backup

Here is the short answer to the question of what to digitize: Anything you can. Even if digital copies are not legally acceptable, you will at least have the information to fill out online forms or re-order the documents as necessary. What if you had to apply for another passport while stuck on vacation?

Once you have digital copies of all these documents, it is also easy to back up your information. I recommend having at least two copies of your files in two separate locations, with one of those locations off-site. That way, you can grab your documents and go if you're at home, or if the worst happens and you cannot access that on-site information, you can access all that information somewhere else.

Is My Digital Go Bag Safe Online?

Good question. This is the most important information in your life. There is a lot you can do to protect yourself, though. You have already achieved one of those things: Setting up a backup strategy. You should also store your data in a secure location. Watch out for clever phishing attempts. And make sure you follow password best practices, including setting up multi-factor authentication (MFA).

Make It a Holiday to Update Your Information Regularly

Just like in the other kits and bags I have asked you to develop, a lot of the information on this list will change over time. Maybe you are the type of person who regularly updates their files, or perhaps you wait for major changes. It's still a good idea to designate one day per year (your birthday, a preferred holiday?) as Update Important Information Day.

Your Turn: There is no sugarcoating this: Digitizing information is a big job. Mark a date on your calendar and at least get started. For now, decide what you are going to do and how you are going to do it, and then put your start date on the calendar and hold yourself accountable to getting started. If a natural disaster destroys your home, you will be glad you did.

Pro Tip: Using an external hard drive and keeping that same hard drive in a safe place outside your home is a great best practice that stores your data somewhere else and keeps it offline.

Resources for Day 5: Your Virtual or Digital Go Bag

There are lots of videos on YouTube that address this subject. This short blog from Prisidio is clear and concise on the topic. https://www.prisidio.com/blog/pack-a-digital-go-bag

PR Daily also has a nice, small guide on digital go bags.

https://www.prdaily.com/is-your-digital-go-bag-ready/

Notes

_____

_____

_____

_____

_____

_____

_____

_____

_____

_____

_____

_____

_____

_____

_____

_____

_____

Day 6
Can You Hear Me Now

The secret of crisis management is not good vs. bad; it's preventing the bad from getting worse.

– Andy Gilman, president & CEO of Comm Core Consulting Group

Day 6 is about your family communication plan. When cellular communication first started, we often asked each other, "Can you hear me now?" The signal clarity was not always reliable, and sometimes, in mid-conversation, you had to confirm you were still talking to someone. Now that cell phones are ubiquitous, we rely heavily on them for everything, which creates a single point of vulnerability in our personal emergency communication planning. The best practice is to have a Primary, Alternate, Contingency, and Emergency plan (PACE plan). This is a tall order that requires careful consideration of what is most practicable. If cellular service is down, how will you communicate? Do you have a list of important phone numbers handy without needing your phone?

Having a plan to communicate with family members when infrastructure goes down is a great way to provide peace of mind, considering the hazards we face today. A plan can also reduce the amount of stress we experience during these types of outages. The **Primary** plan is what you do when the world is operating as normal, with no interruptions to power grids or communications systems. An example of a primary plan would be to use your cell phone to call a family member. **Alternate** plans are methods of communication that, although not as convenient or effective as the primary option, are still viable alternatives. An example of an alternate plan is to use social media, email, or phone service applications like "WhatsApp" (and many others) to contact a family member. **Contingency** plans come into play if primary and alternate methods fail. This solution is not as convenient as the first two options. In this scenario, the cell phone networks and the internet are likely down. An example of a contingency plan is to use pre-purchased radios or walkie-talkies to communicate. The last step in PACE planning is the **Emergency** method. This is your last-ditch plan. Nothing else has worked, and you need to think out of the box. In this scenario, your last-ditch effort might be to meet your family members at a pre-arranged park if that is the closest point to your workplace. If one person doesn't show up, consider leaving a note in a pre-determined location at the park and heading home.

So, considering the points above, a basic PACE plan for your family could look like this:

1. Primary – cell phone or text message

2. Alternate – social media or email that your whole family uses
3. Contingency – GMRS radio or family walkie-talkie
4. Emergency – Meet up in person at a pre-arranged location

You would then add more detail and context around each of these categories, such as specifying a group for texting, addresses for social media, channels for radios and walkie-talkies, and a location to meet up. When working on your PACE plan, try to avoid having a single point of failure. If all your plans rely on the internet, then you are vulnerable to internet failures. PACE plans should be reviewed and updated regularly to reflect changes in addresses, channels, personnel, and phone numbers. Instructions can be printed on a wallet-sized card and given to each person. When possible, have an out-of-town point of contact, such as a friend or relative, who can relay your messages. This is a person you can use for coordination when you cannot get through to others or local communication systems are saturated.

Your Turn: Start your family's PACE plan. It doesn't have to be perfect at first, but jumping into this task is important for your own resilience and growth. Act and get started.

Pro Tip: Involve your whole family in this process. Teenagers communicate differently from grandparents. Work through the preferences and then practice your PACE plan with family communications drills to see if everyone can complete all four steps, eventually memorizing them.

Resources for Day 6: Can You Hear Me Now?

U.S. Federal Emergency Management Agency (FEMA) Family Communication Planning
https://www.ready.gov/sites/default/files/2020-03/familyemergency-communication-planning-document.pdf

Habitat for Humanity Family Communications Plan
https://www.habitat.org/our-work/disasterresponse/disaster-preparedness-homeowners/familycommunications-plan

Guardian Protection Family Communication Plan

https://guardianprotection.com/blog/this-family-emergency-communication-plan-will-help-you-protect-the-ones-you-love-free-template/

Notes

_____

_____

_____

_____

_____

_____

_____

_____

_____

_____

_____

_____

_____

_____

_____

_____

_____

_____

Day 7
Know Your Risks

Risk assessment should be an ongoing process to stay ahead of potential threats.

– Statement found in many business classes.

So far, we have been working on basic emergency preparedness planning, and we have even put some of our planning into action. Because we have not discussed preparing for anything specific, you might be asking yourself, "What are we preparing for, exactly?' Preparing for a broad range of potential threats, rather than focusing on specific ones, is called "All Hazards Planning," a term emergency managers and other public safety officials use to describe general emergency planning. Rather than preparing for dozens of specific threats, which can be overwhelming, we should focus on completing our basic emergency planning to address at least eighty-five percent of the problem before delving into specifics. All-hazards planning helps us mitigate our personal risk. Risk management and risk assessment can be very complicated topics at the corporate level or when managing an organization or business. We have often heard of SWOT diagrams that help us determine strengths, weaknesses, opportunities, and threats. There are also theoretical mathematical formulas to help us quantify risk, such as

Risk = Likelihood x Impact or

Risk = Threat x Vulnerability x Consequence

Risk management is so broad that you can take entire graduate school programs and business continuity certification classes on the determination of risk. We do not want to make it that complicated! What are the natural emergencies that can happen in your area? The list could potentially be quite long. Rather than just guessing or relying on the recent past or what has happened in your area during your lifetime, consult local planning documents readily available online at the town, city, county, state, and regional levels. Professionals build these products with groups of engineers, urban planners, flood plain managers, meteorologists, emergency managers, and many more. Sometimes these are called "THIRAS" or Threat Hazard Identification Risk Assessments. These helpful documents are updated periodically and will tell you about the probability and severity of potential hazards in your area. Much of this you know already through experience, but what we are trying to understand is our true risk and vulnerabilities, and not just how we "feel" about things. Our own psychological foibles can steer us in the wrong direction or fail to indicate a low-probability, high-consequence threat in our area that we may have overlooked. For example, if you live in a seismically prone area, you may not even realize it or consider it if an earthquake has not happened in the last fifty years.

Your Turn: Assess the top five natural hazard risks in your area on your own. Include anything and everything safety-related that concerns you. Include natural emergencies only for now. Then, consult a professionally prepared risk assessment of where you live. Consider using the United States National Risk Index below, if appropriate for you. How did they match? Your assessment is not "wrong" if different. It is your own perception, and that is fine. If tornadoes concern you, make them part of your planning, regardless of the official index, because "low" threat does not mean "no" threat generally. Write down your Top Five natural emergencies for planning purposes in the notes section of this chapter.

Pro Tip: Consult a hazard vulnerability map for your area. Separately, look at a flood plain map for your area. While you may not live in an area prone to flooding, your house or neighborhood could be in a smaller area that has that danger, such as in a lower elevation, a valley, or next to a river.

Resources for Day 7: Know Your Risk

United States National Risk Index

https://hazards.fema.gov/nri/

Notes

_____

_____

_____

_____

_____

_____

_____

_____

_____

_____

Day 8
Hurricanes

I'll never forget Hurricane Katrina – the mix of a natural disaster and a man-made catastrophe that resulted in the death of over 1,500 of our neighbors. Millions of folks were marked by the tragedy.

– Cedric Richmond

Now that we have learned the concept of all-hazards planning on Day 7, we'll focus on some of the most frequent hazards found around the world. If hurricanes do not pertain to your current living situation, they could during a vacation or business trip. There is nothing "good" about a hurricane, but it is one of the few hazards that gives us several days' warning before making landfall. Hurricanes are massive storm systems that form over the water and move toward land. Threats from hurricanes include high winds, heavy rainfall, storm surge, coastal and inland flooding, rip currents, and tornadoes. These large storms are called typhoons in the North Pacific Ocean and cyclones in other parts of the world. Hurricanes can cause loss of life and catastrophic damage to property along coastlines and can extend several hundred miles inland. The extent of damage varies according to the size and wind intensity of the storm, the amount and duration of rainfall, the path of the storm, and other factors such as the number and type of buildings in the area, the terrain, and soil conditions. While storms are tracked as soon as they have the potential to become a tropical cyclone, it is difficult to predict the path of the storm far in advance. Forecasters generally identify a cone or a range to illustrate the path that the storm may take. People who live in hurricane-prone coastal areas should know their vulnerability to wind and flooding, as well as what to do to reduce the effects of both. People who live inland from coastal areas may also experience high winds, power outages, and flooding from torrential rain. Protecting yourself today involves several key steps: having access to reliable information sources, preparing your home or workplace, developing an emergency communications plan (see Day 6), and knowing what to do when a hurricane approaches your community. Acting today can save lives and property. Once an alert or warning is issued for your area, closely follow the information on the news or a weather radio, and get updates from the National Weather Service (in the United States). A few days before a hurricane is a great time to check your go-bag and shelter-in-place supplies and replace or restock as needed. Bring inside anything that can be picked up by the wind (bicycles, lawn furniture) because these things turn into deadly projectiles. Close windows, doors, and hurricane shutters. If you do not have hurricane shutters, close and board up all windows and doors with plywood. Turn the refrigerator and freezer to the coldest setting and keep them closed as much as possible so that food will last longer if the power goes out. Turn off propane tanks and unplug small appliances. Fill your car's gas tank in case you must evacuate and travel beyond your immediate area.

Talk with members of your household and update your evacuation plan. (Day 28). Planning and practicing your evacuation plan will minimize confusion and fear during the event. Learn about your community's hurricane response plan. Plan routes to local shelters, register family members with special medical needs as required, and make plans for your pets to be cared for (Day 24). Evacuate if advised by authorities. Be careful to avoid flooded roads and washed-out bridges. Because standard homeowner's insurance doesn't cover flooding, it is essential to have protection from the floods associated with hurricanes, tropical storms, heavy rains, and other conditions that impact the U.S. On a final note, hurricanes are unique in the pantheon of disasters in that many learn the wrong lessons from surviving them. Routinely, folks who live in hurricane-prone areas become loath to evacuate the more they survive. "We'll be okay. We made it through the last one." "The forecasters get this wrong. They always miss us." Take every hurricane seriously and do not let this poorly formulated, incongruent thinking happen to you. If a hurricane does miss you, use it as a training and planning opportunity anyway. Please do not have a "hurricane party" instead.

Your Turn: Consider using the United States National Risk Index for hurricanes below if appropriate for you. What is the risk of hurricanes where you live? Is there a higher risk where you vacation or visit family members? Write these risk levels down in the notes page of this chapter.

Pro Tip: Purchase a NOAA (National Oceanic and Atmospheric Administration) approved weather radio. You can set an alert for your area that triggers a warning and "wakes up" the radio when there are important bulletins.

Resources for Day 8: for Hurricanes:

For more information on flood insurance in the U.S., please visit the National Flood Insurance Program Website.
www.FloodSmart.gov

United States National Risk Index for Hurricanes

https://hazards.fema.gov/nri/hurricane

National Oceanic and Atmospheric Administration (NOAA) Hurricane Preparedness

https://www.noaa.gov/hurricane-prep

Notes

_____

_____

_____

_____

_____

_____

_____

_____

_____

_____

Day 9 Flooding

Floods are "acts of God," but flood losses are largely acts of man.

– Gilbert F. White

Now that we have learned the concept of all-hazards planning on Day 7 and hurricanes on Day 8, we will focus on what is sometimes a byproduct of hurricanes and one of the most pervasive and destructive hazards in the world: flooding. Flooding is the most common natural disaster in the United States and can happen anywhere. Flooding ranks with hurricanes and earthquakes in terms of death and property damage each year globally. If flooding does not pertain to your current living situation, it could during a vacation or business trip. Flooding is an overflowing of water onto land that is usually dry. Flooding may happen with only a few inches of water, or it may cover a house to the rooftop. Flooding can occur during any season, but some areas of the United States are at greater risk at certain times of the year. Coastal areas are at greater risk for flooding during hurricane season (i.e., June to November), while the Midwest is more at risk in the spring and during heavy summer rains. Ice jams occur in the spring in the Northeast and Northwest. Even the deserts of the Southwest are at risk during the late summer monsoon season. Flooding can happen in any U.S. state or territory. It is imperative to be prepared for flooding if you live in a low-lying area near a body of water (such as a river, stream, or culvert), along a coast, or downstream from a dam or levee.

When preparing for a flood, listen to the news on area radio and television stations. Stay informed about flooding in your area, as some flooding is highly localized. Be prepared to evacuate at a moment's notice (See Day 28). Well before the flood, update go-bags (See Day 2) and family communication plans (See Day 6). Like almost all other emergencies, there may not be time to do this after a warning is issued. When a flood or flash flood warning is issued in your area, head for higher ground and stay there. Stay away from flood waters. If you come upon a flowing stream where water is above your ankles, stop, turn around, and go another way.

The national campaign of "Turn Around, Don't Drown" highlights the fact that many are overconfident about the depth of flood waters when not knowing about sudden changes in the landscape below the waterline or sharp debris in the water. This is especially true when driving, as it takes only a few inches of water for some vehicles to lose traction and start floating. If you are caught on a flooded road and waters are rising rapidly around you, get out of the car quickly and move to higher ground. Most cars can be swept away by less than two feet of moving water. Keep children out of the water. They are curious and often lack judgment about running water or contaminated water. Be especially cautious at night when it is harder to recognize flood danger. Because standard homeowner's insurance does not cover flooding, it is important to have protection from the floods associated with hurricanes, tropical storms, heavy rains, and other conditions. Do your best to stay out of floodwater altogether. First responders have often been chemically burned from helping in floods. Everything that can be found on dry land is now in the water. This includes medical waste, raw sewage, and dead animals.

Your Turn: Consider using the United States National Risk Index for floods below if appropriate for you. What is the risk of floods where you live? Is there a higher risk where you vacation or visit family members? Write these risk levels down in the notes page of this chapter.

Pro Tip: Purchase a NOAA (National Oceanic and Atmospheric Administration) approved weather radio. You can set an alert for your area that triggers a warning and "wakes up" the radio when there are essential bulletins. Your NOAA radio will inform you of possible flood warnings and reports of flooding in progress or other critical information from the National Weather Service (NWS).

Resources for Day 9: Flooding

For more information on flood insurance in the U.S., please visit the National Flood Insurance Program Website.

www.FloodSmart.gov

United States National Risk Index (in the upper left of the hazard index, consult both coastal and riverine flooding).

https://hazards.fema.gov/nri/map

American Red Cross Flood Preparedness

https://www.redcross.org/get-help/how-to-prepare-foremergencies/types-of-emergencies/flood.html

U.S. National Weather Service Flood Safety

https://www.weather.gov/safety/flood-before

Notes

Day 10
Severe Storms

There's no such thing as bad weather, just soft people.

– Bill Bowerman

Have you ever been caught in a rain shower, only to have it turn more severe than expected within minutes, resulting in a full-blown thunderstorm? It is scary and can become dangerous quite quickly. For the purposes of our Day 10 discussion, we will use the U.S. National Weather Service (NWS) definition of a severe thunderstorm, which produces hail at least an inch in diameter, winds of 58 miles per hour or stronger, or a tornado. This discussion will also include lightning because lightning is generally associated with these storms, and a lightning strike can kill you. A thunderstorm affects a relatively small area when compared to a hurricane or a winter storm. The typical thunderstorm is 15 miles in diameter and will last an average of 30 minutes. Despite their small size, ALL thunderstorms are dangerous! Of the estimated 100,000 thunderstorms that occur each year in the United States, about 10 percent are classified as severe. You need to get inside a sturdy building before a thunderstorm hits. A sturdy building is a structure with walls and a foundation. Once you have identified a sturdy building, plan to shelter in the basement or a small, interior, windowless room on the lowest level to provide additional protection from high winds. Plan to stay inside until weather forecasts indicate it is safe to leave. Mobile, manufactured, trailer homes, and recreational vehicles (RVs) are not safe in high winds. If you live in one of these structures, identify a sturdy building nearby that you can quickly access.

Practice drills with everyone in your household, so everyone knows where to go and what to do before a thunderstorm hits. Completing the preparations made on Days 1 through 7 before the storm will be crucial to your success. Pay attention to weather alerts and local information. Postpone outdoor activities if the forecast calls for thunderstorms. Do not just "push through it." Remember, no place outside is safe when thunderstorms are in the area. If you are caught outside in a thunderstorm, keep moving toward a secure shelter. Sheds, gazebos, dugouts, and bleachers do not protect from lightning and high winds. It is dangerous to take refuge under a tree, as it is the leading cause of death from lightning strikes. You could also be killed or injured by strong winds blowing down trees and branches. Being in a vehicle is safer than being outside; however, if you have time, drive to the closest sturdy building and take shelter inside. If you are driving and cannot get to a sturdy structure, pull off the road and park in a place where falling trees and power lines will not hit you. As mentioned on Day 9, flash flooding happens quickly. Move to higher ground before floodwater reaches you. Never walk, swim, or drive through floodwater. Turn around! Don't drown!

Special Notes on Lightning. As previously mentioned, there is no safe place outdoors when a thunderstorm is nearby. Although rare, lightning can be dangerous even when you are inside. Most lightning victims were going to a safe place, but waited too long before seeking shelter. As a storm approaches, many people may assume lightning is too far away to pose any danger, but it can travel as far as ten miles from a thunderstorm. If you are close enough to the storm to hear thunder, then you are close enough to be struck by lightning. A darkening cloud is often the first sign that lightning may strike. As soon as you see lightning or hear thunder, move indoors quickly and stay away from windows, plumbing, and electrical devices. If you are caught outside when lightning occurs, the most dangerous place to be is an open area. When a substantial building is not available and there is imminent lightning, get into a hard-topped vehicle, but remember to keep your hands and feet away from the side of the car, as well as the dashboard, steering wheel, and windows. Outdoor water activities such as swimming, boating, and fishing are also very dangerous during lightning. Be sure to head back to land as soon as bad weather threatens. Most people struck by lightning are not killed but suffer significant injuries. Remember that a lightning victim does not continue to carry an electrical charge and should begin receiving emergency medical care immediately. Simply not going outside during a thunderstorm is your best defense from lightning.

Your Turn: What is the risk of severe storms and lightning where you live? Is there a higher risk where you vacation or visit family members? Write these risk levels down in the notes page of this chapter. Discuss what you have done to prepare for severe storms with your family, friends, neighbors, and colleagues.

Pro Tip: When you make your severe storm plan, make sure to conduct a drill with your family and practice your plan. This will create a better understanding of the plan and start to produce a level of resilience for you and others. To paraphrase the words of Amanda Ripley, author of *The Unthinkable,* psychologically, you are not only preparing to survive but to thrive on the other end of a major disaster.

Resources for Day 10: Severe Storms

United States National Risk Index (in the upper left of the hazard index consult tornado).

https://hazards.fema.gov/nri/map

Learn how to protect your property from high winds.

https://www.fema.gov/sites/default/files/202011/fema_protect-your-property_severe-wind.pdf

Learn about emotional distress caused by severe storms.

https://www.samhsa.gov/mental-health/disasterpreparedness/disaster-types/tornadoes

U.S. National Weather Service Severe Storm and Hail Safety

https://www.weather.gov/mlb/hail_rules

Nationwide Insurance Hail Safety

https://www.nationwide.com/lc/resources/emergencypreparedness/articles/hail

U.S. Centers for Disease Control Lightning Safety

https://www.cdc.gov/lightning/safety/index.html

Notes

_____

_____

_____

_____

_____

_____

_____

_____

_____

Day 11
Tornadoes

Today, technology is there to give early and normally ample warning when a powerful tornado approaches. When a tornado strikes, all of us are at risk

–Spencer Bachus

I have separated tornadoes from Day 10 Severe Storms because they are nature's most violent storms and demand careful preparation from everyone. As mentioned previously, they come from powerful thunderstorms. They appear as a funnel- or cone-shaped cloud with winds that can reach up to 300 miles per hour. They cause damage when they touch the ground, potentially affecting an area one mile wide and 50 miles long. Before tornadoes hit, the wind may die down, and the air may become very still. Having advance notice that a tornado is approaching your area can give you the critical time needed to move to a place with better protection. Pay attention to weather reports and sign up for text alerts and smartphone apps that provide weather warnings. It is important to remember that you may not always receive an official tornado alert in your area. You may need to use your judgment to seek protection when you see or hear a dangerous storm advancing. Know the tornado warning signs. Look up! If you see any of the danger signs, take shelter immediately. These include a dark or green colored sky, large, dark, low-lying clouds, large hail, and possibly a loud roar like a freight train. To ensure that you can act quickly and get the best protection available during a tornado, you need to plan. (See Day 10) There are steps you can take right now to lower the risk for you and your loved ones. Planning and practicing specifically how and where you take cover for protection may save your life. Know the areas that are prone to frequent and severe tornadoes. Learn whether you live, work, or travel through areas that are prone to frequent and severe tornadoes. Know how to stay informed. Identify the locations where you spend a lot of time, such as home, work, school, or house of worship, and determine the highest available level of protection from a tornado. With the devastation potential of a tornado, we can see the utility of all-hazards planning and the individual work we have done thus far on Days 1 - 7. First responders will be overwhelmed by a large multi-jurisdictional tornado, and you may be on your own for quite some time when dealing with the aftermath of such a large disaster.

Your Turn: What is the risk of tornadoes where you live? Is there a higher risk where you vacation or visit family members? Write these risk levels down in the notes page of this chapter. Discuss what you have done to prepare for a tornado with your family, friends, neighbors, and colleagues.

Pro Tip: Now that you have made a severe storm plan, add the idea of a tornado to your planning and make sure to conduct a drill with your family and practice your plan. Plans mean very little without practice and a drill.

Resources for Day 11: Tornadoes

United States National Risk Index (in the upper left of the hazard index consult tornado).

https://hazards.fema.gov/nri/map

The U.S. National Weather Service has great information for tornado preparedness.

https://www.weather.gov/safety/tornado-prepare

American Red Cross Tornado Safety Tips

https://www.redcross.org/get-help/how-to-prepare-for-emergencies/types-of-emergencies/tornado.html

U.S. Federal Emergency Management Agency (FEMA) tornado preparedness

https://www.ready.gov/tornadoes

Learn how to protect your property from high winds.

https://www.fema.gov/sites/default/files/2020-11/fema_protect-your-property_severe-wind.pdf

Learn about emotional distress caused by severe storms.

https://www.samhsa.gov/mental-health/disaster-preparedness/disaster-types/tornadoes

U.S. Centers for Disease Control Tornado Preparedness

https://www.cdc.gov/tornadoes/about/

Notes

_____

_____

_____

_____

_____

_____

_____

_____

Day 12
Water Safety

Drowning is the second leading cause of unintentional injury death for children ages 1 to 14 years, and the fifth leading cause for people of all ages

–U.S. Centers for Disease Control

Thus far, all the hazards we have discussed involve water. We can now discuss a broad general point in daily living preparedness: water safety. Learning basic swimming is an important life-saving skill for everyone. Having a small accident that involves falling into the water should be humorous and not life-threatening. Imagine being trapped in a dangerous situation surrounded by water, unable to float or propel yourself to safety? Many of us enjoy the ocean, going to the beach, swimming in a pool, lake, or river, kayaking, canoeing, and fishing. You name the activity, and water can be fun for everybody. Water also kills indiscriminately regardless of age, sex, background, or citizenship. Drowning is a serious threat. It is the third largest cause of accidental death in the world. Additionally, we naturally think that those who are swimming or fishing are the most susceptible to drowning. Not true! People who have gone out walking or jogging are at far greater risk than others. Feeling a little worried after reading that?

There is plenty of information about this topic, but one of the best resources is the West Mercia Search and Rescue

Organization's course "Home and Dry: No More River Deaths." (See Resources below.) This free course from our friends in the United Kingdom is available online, complete with great videos, or it can be downloaded as a PDF for personal viewing or for presenting to another group. West Mercia breaks down the fundamentals of water safety by providing an overview of the science, problems, and solutions to various situations from a layperson's perspective. Most importantly, the course walks you through some simple problem prevention techniques, what to do in different kinds of water emergencies, and "how to look after your mates" with this fine contribution to the English language: "If your mate's on the beer, keep them well clear." Great advice indeed! Lastly, West Mercia recognizes that even after all you have done to prevent or address a problem, you still might have to rescue someone, with "Talk, Reach, Throw" being the basic sequence of priorities. Their website uses the "Shout, Reach, Throw" model, whereas in the United States, we adopted "Reach, Throw, Row, Go" -which is now being revised doctrinally to end with "Don't Go." Regardless, the key takeaway is for the rescuer to consider the increased risk while prioritizing their safety, as creating additional victims is of no benefit. The course also addresses first aid through recovery position, rescue breaths, and chest compressions. Its comprehensive content makes it a one- stop resource for water safety applicable to everyone--especially if you are taking your family or a group to a water destination. This course not only reviews material you already know about, but it also introduces new information, making it one of the most comprehensive water safety courses available.

Your Turn: Take the West Mercia and Rescue Organization "Home and Dry: No More River Deaths" course as soon as possible. It is only thirty minutes or so and will make you and your family much safer around the water.

Pro Tip: Life jackets save lives—bring one if they will not be readily available on your outing. Lifeguards may not be present; know if they are on duty. Bring essential gear for boats or vessels, such as navigational devices and paddle floats. People have different comfort levels with water. We can be safer together. When enjoying water activities with children, designate a water watcher. There are drownings each year in the presence of many people.

Resources for Day 12: Water Safety

West Mercia Search and Rescue Organization and their free course entitled "Home and Dry: No More River Deaths."

https://westmerciasar.org.uk/

https://westmerciasar.org.uk/homeanddry/

American Red Cross Water Safety

https://www.redcross.org/get-help/how-to-prepare-for-emergencies/types-of-emergencies/water-safety.html

Splash Forward Water Safety Resources

https://splashforward.org/water-safety-resources/

Notes

_____

_____

_____

_____

_____

_____

_____

_____

_____

Day 13
Earthquakes

We cannot stop natural disasters, but we can arm ourselves with knowledge: so many lives would not have to be lost if there were enough disaster preparedness.

–Petra Nemcova

Like the water-related hazards we have explored, earthquakes are some of the most frequent hazards found around the world. If earthquakes do not pertain to your current living situation, they could during a vacation or business trip. An earthquake is the sudden, rapid shaking of the earth, caused by the breaking and shifting of subterranean rock as it releases strain that has accumulated over a long time. Initial mild shaking may strengthen and become extremely violent within seconds. Additional earthquakes, called aftershocks, may occur for hours, days, or even months. Most are smaller than the initial earthquake, but larger magnitude aftershocks also occur. You may experience shaking or a rolling motion in the walls, floor, or ground. This movement may grow more extreme within seconds. If you do not drop down immediately, you may be knocked off your feet. You may not be able to walk or run. Objects may fall off shelves, and light fixtures may swing or fall from ceilings, or tall furniture may fall over. There may be dust or glass particles in the air or on the ground. You may hear noises like a heavy truck or train passing nearby. As described, earthquakes are particularly terrifying. The national campaign of DROP! COVER! HOLD ON! is a great device to help us remember what to do in the initial moment of an earthquake. Most casualties and injuries from earthquakes occur when people run outside and heavy objects fall on them. So, while there are innumerable different circumstances you may find yourself in when an earthquake strikes, be ready to be flexible and prepare ahead of time. Earthquakes require their specific preparations. First, become aware of fire evacuation and earthquake plans for all the buildings you occupy regularly. Having this immediate knowledge could save your life. Panic creates hesitation, and in this case, hesitation kills. Next, pick safe places in each room of your home, workplace, and school. A safe place could be under a piece of furniture or against an interior wall away from windows, bookcases, or tall furniture that could fall on you. Importantly, practice the drop, cover, and hold procedure in each safe place. We're striving for "muscle memory" here in terms of training ourselves to have an automatic response. If you don't have sturdy furniture to hold onto, sit on the floor next to an interior wall and cover your head and neck with your arms. Also, keep a flashlight and sturdy shoes by each person's bed. This will help to make quick, positive decisions with the right tools. While planning for earthquakes, familiarize yourself with some construction aspects of your home and make sure your home is securely anchored to its foundation. Bolt and brace water heaters and gas appliances to wall studs. Bolt bookcases, cabinets, and other tall furniture to wall studs. Additionally,

Hang heavy items, such as pictures and mirrors, away from beds, couches, and anywhere people sleep or sit. While you are securing things, remember to brace overhead light fixtures. Lastly, and this is a real lifesaver, learn how to shut off the gas valves, water, and electricity in your home and keep tools handy for those purposes. Maintaining your previous preparations from Days 1-7 will be critically important during an earthquake. It might take days to restore critical infrastructure and basic supplies. As with all disasters and emergencies, your level of preparedness will determine your quality of life in the weeks and months that follow. As you reconsider your planning for earthquakes, adjust your overall plan and communications. Put your go-bag and other disaster preparedness items in convenient locations. Minimize financial hardships by organizing important documents, strengthening your property, and considering insurance needs. (Days 5 and 20).

Remember the national campaign of DROP! COVER! HOLD ON! When an earthquake strikes. Improve safety after earthquakes by evacuating, if necessary (Day 28), helping the injured (Day 19), and preventing further injuries or damage. Restore daily life by reconnecting with others, repairing damage, and rebuilding community (Day 30).

Your Turn: Earthquakes are a special hazard that requires unique preparations beyond our simple all-hazards preparedness. Take the precautions above if you live in a seismically prone area. Act and get started. Do not put it off.

Pro Tip: Register for the "Great Shake Out below, which takes place every year in October in the United States. Get your whole family and community involved!

Resources for Day 13: Earthquakes

United States National Risk Index for Earthquakes (go to the upper left corner and search earthquake).

https://hazards.fema.gov/nri/map

Center for Disease Control Earthquake Preparedness

https://www.cdc.gov/earthquakes/safety/stay-safe-during-an-earthquake.html

"Great Shake Out" Earthquake Preparedness campaign

https://www.shakeout.org

American Red Cross Earthquake Safety

https://www.redcross.org/get-help/how-to-prepare-for-emergencies/types-of-emergencies/earthquake.html

Notes

_____

_____

_____

_____

_____

_____

_____

_____

_____

Day 14
Wildfires

Due to climate change, wildfires are growing in size, frequency, and intensity, and wildfire seasons are becoming longer.

–Mikie Sherrill

Wildfires are increasing globally. If they do not pertain to your current living situation, they could during a vacation or business trip. Wildfire is an unplanned, unwanted fire burning in a natural area, such as a forest, grassland, or prairie. As building development expands into these areas, homes and businesses may be situated in or near areas susceptible to wildfires. This is called the wildland urban interface. Wildfire can damage natural resources, destroy homes, and threaten the safety of the public and the firefighters who protect forests and communities. A small localized wildfire is possible almost anywhere, so you might be more susceptible to it than you think. The United States National Weather Service (NWS) of the National Oceanic and Atmospheric Administration (NOAA) issues notices when weather conditions such as strong winds, low relative humidity, and high temperatures make wildfires more likely. During these dangerous periods, NWS urges everyone to use extreme caution because a simple spark can cause a major wildfire. Act now! Protecting yourself today involves several key steps: having access to reliable information sources, preparing your home or workplace, developing an emergency communications plan, and knowing what to do when a wildfire approaches your home or community. Acting today can save lives and property. Sign up for your community's warning system. As mentioned previously, the Emergency Alert System (EAS) and NOAA Weather Radio also provide emergency alerts. By knowing your community's evacuation routes (See Day 28), you may find several ways to leave the area. Once you have several alternatives, drive the evacuation routes and find shelter locations.

Animals of all sorts are particularly vulnerable to wildfire. Make sure to have a plan for pets and livestock (See Day 24). Gather emergency supplies and complete the planning found in Days 1-7. Be sure to include N95 respirator masks that filter out particles in the air from dust and smoke. Evacuating due to wildfire will depend on the location of the fire and prevailing winds. When it is time to evacuate, do so immediately with the planning found in Day 28 while keeping in mind each person's specific needs, including medication (See Day 24). Sadly, in a wildfire, you may not return for a very long time, if at all. This could imply the complete destruction of your community and home. Make sure to keep essential documents in a fireproof safe if you cannot take them with you, and update your Digital Go-Bag from Day 5. Mitigation is just as important as other preparedness activities for wildfire. In terms of the construction of your home, use fire-resistant materials to build, renovate, or make repairs. Also, find an outdoor water source with a hose that can reach any area of your property in case it is safe to fight the fire and keep your home from burning. Consider your landscaping as well, by creating a fire-resistant zone that is free of leaves, debris, or flammable materials for at least thirty feet from your home. Review your insurance coverage to ensure it is sufficient to replace your property (Day 20). In addition to the great general preparedness you have completed thus far, during periods of heightened alert, back vehicles into your garage or park them in an open space facing the direction of escape. Keep the gas tank in vehicles at least half full. As noted before, drilling your plans is key to positive outcomes. Practice often with everyone in your home, using at least two ways out of your neighborhood.

Your Turn: Wildfires are a special hazard that requires unique preparations beyond our simple all-hazards preparedness. If you live in a wildfire-prone area, act and get started. Do not put it off.

Pro Tip: Make sure you understand the wildfire risk for where you live based on the United States National Risk Index below. Participate in community wildfire drills. If something could keep you from leaving successfully, such as a locked gate, address it immediately. Practice evacuating animals and pets, including how to operate trailers and other vehicles needed to transport them.

Resources for Day 14: Wildfires

United States National Risk Index for Wildfire (go to the upper left corner and search wildfire).

https://hazards.fema.gov/nri/map

Centers for Disease Control: Preparing for Wildfires

https://www.cdc.gov/wildfires/safety/index.html

American Red Cross Wildfire Safety

https://www.redcross.org/get-help/how-to-prepare-for-emergencies/types-of-emergencies/wildfire.html

National Weather Service Wildland Fire Safety

https://www.weather.gov/safety/wildfire-ready

U.S. Forest Service Wildfire Risk to Communities

https://wildfirerisk.org/reduce-risk/evacuation-readiness/

Notes

_____

_____

_____

_____

_____

_____

_____

_____

_____

Day 15
Home Fire

A house on fire is not just an emergency; it is a moment that defines who we are in the face of disaster.

–Anonymous

Any building can have a fire. In only a matter of minutes, a small house fire can rage out of control. Heat temperatures from a building fire can reach up to 1,500°F. The flames emit carbon monoxide gas, which is odorless, colorless, and tasteless – and can cause immediate unconsciousness, followed by death. Every family should have and practice a home escape plan to follow in the event of a fire. The plan should include several key steps: drawing a diagram of your home to mark the locations of windows and doors, planning two escape routes out of every room, setting up a meeting place outside the home for everyone to gather after an escape, and practicing the escape plan once a month. Every member of the family and frequent visitors to the home should know and practice the escape route.

The Federal Emergency Management Agency (FEMA) stresses that even children as young as three years old can understand an escape plan. Fire safety is not complicated, and it is our responsibility. Complete a home fire safety checklist and identify fire risks in your home. Test smoke alarms and carbon monoxide detectors monthly and change the batteries at least once a year. Place smoke alarms on each floor of your home and in each bedroom. Make sure that everyone in the home can hear the smoke alarm from their bedrooms. Make a family fire escape plan and practice it once a month. Make sure that everyone in the house understands the family fire escape plan. If your home has more than one floor, ensure you understand the fire escape plans and exits, or have the necessary equipment to exit through windows safely. Place fire extinguishers throughout your home and make sure everyone in the house knows how to use them. Ensure there is a fire extinguisher on each floor of the home. Never leave food unattended on the stove, keep all matches and lighters out of the reach of children, and do not place portable heaters near flammable materials.

Your Turn: Create your own home escape plan using the notes page and grid plan provided at the end of this chapter. Understand fire safety protocols for fires where you work and at schools where family members attend. Participate actively in all drills. Act and get started. Do not put it off.

Pro Tip: Know the number for the local fire department and give them a call about fire safety and the use of extinguishers. They will be happy to help you! Attend fire safety events offered by the local fire department in your area.

Resources for Day 15: Home Fire

U.S. Fire Administration Escape Plans

https://www.usfa.fema.gov/prevention/home-fires/prepare-for-fire/home-fire-escape-plans/

Federal Emergency Management Agency (FEMA) Fire Escape Plans

https://www.ready.gov/home-fire-escape-plan

American Red Cross Fire Safety

https://www.redcross.org/get-help/how-to-prepare-for-emergencies/types-of-emergencies/fire.html

The U.S. National Fire Prevention Association has Fire Prevention Week every October in the United States.

https://www.nfpa.org/events/fire-prevention-week

U.S. Fire Administration Fire Safety for Children

https://www.usfa.fema.gov/prevention/home-fires/at-risk-audiences/children/

Safe Kids Worldwide - Fire

https://www.safekids.org/fire

Notes

Day 16
Human-Caused Disasters

Our problems are man-made; therefore, they may be solved by man. And man can be as big as he wants. No problem of human destiny is beyond human beings.

–John F. Kennedy

Man-made or human-caused disasters fit in the "all others" category, which is extensive. I do not want to make Day 16 complicated with over-categorization because there is a lot of overlap here with different types of accidents writ large in the areas of industrial, transportation, and construction. Crime, attacks, arson, civil disorder, terrorism, war, biological, chemical, and radiological threats also fit into this area, as do public health hazards. I will address long-term power outages and cyber preparedness in Days 17 and 18. Do not get overwhelmed by a long list of things that could happen to you! We have discussed natural hazards in detail and focused on some specific ones on Days 8 through 15. But this is where we put what we learned on Day 7 about knowing your risks to the test. Just like we did for natural disasters, consult local planning documents readily available online at the town, city, county, state, and regional levels to understand human-made hazards in your area. Professionals build these products with groups of engineers, urban planners, flood plain managers, meteorologists, emergency managers, and many more. Sometimes these are called "THIRAS" or Threat Hazard Identification Risk Assessments. With human-caused emergencies, you may have to dig a little deeper and use basic observation.

Do you live on the flight path of a major airport? Do you live near a large highway or railway where hazardous materials are transported? How far away is the closest nuclear power plant? Is there an oil refinery in your area? Is there an outbreak of an illness that is starting to make the news in your area? It is worth noting that most disasters have cascading effects, such as flooding causing chemical spills and earthquakes triggering fires, among other consequences. Any disaster can eventually create a public health hazard if not appropriately addressed. Note that thorough hazard planning goes a long way in preparing for almost anything. If you find something in the list above or something specific to your situation, you should prepare for it.

Notes on Chemical and Hazardous Materials: Small, localized hazardous material spills are more pervasive than people think, which is why almost every metropolitan area has a hazardous material (HAZMAT) response unit or at least trained personnel. Hazardous materials can include explosives, flammable and combustible substances, poisons, and radioactive materials. Chemical agents are poisonous vapors, aerosols, liquids, and solids that have toxic effects on people, animals, or plants. Emergencies can happen during production, storage, transportation, use, or disposal of hazardous materials. You are at risk when chemicals are used unsafely or released in harmful amounts, where you live, work, or play. Signs of a chemical release include difficulty breathing, eye irritation, loss of coordination, nausea, or burning in the nose, throat, and lungs. The presence of many dead insects or birds may indicate a chemical or chemical agent release. Many communities have Local Emergency Planning Committees (LEPCs) responsible for collecting information about chemicals and hazardous materials in the community and planning for accidents. These materials are available to the public upon request. Contact your local emergency management office for more information on LEPCs.

Notes on Group Violence: In times of widespread political demonstrations and civil unrest, your best course of action is to avoid any areas where marches and similar activities may occur. If, however, you find yourself caught up in a protest and are worried about your safety, a few precautions can help you avoid the worst and get home safely. During times of political uncertainty, it is crucial to keep an eye on the news. Large-scale demonstrations are generally announced days or even weeks in advance. Knowing this can help you avoid the affected areas. If a large-scale demonstration is expected, your best course of action is to stay home and avoid the area altogether. If you must leave home, make sure you plan multiple routes to and from your destination. You never know which streets or public transportation lines may be affected. Keep in mind that demonstrations can take place with little or no notice and, in extreme cases, quickly turn violent. Exercise caution if you find yourself unexpectedly in the vicinity of large gatherings. In such situations, always be aware of your surroundings. If suddenly surrounded by a crowd, avoid confrontation by keeping your head down and moving with the flow of people. While keeping a low profile, seek an avenue of escape. Do not run or panic. If you are with loved ones, hold hands or lock elbows. Pick up the children to prevent them from being trampled. Staying together is a priority. If you find yourself in the middle of the crowd, move toward the outside and away from any excitement or activity. Once you find an opening, walk away from the crowd as calmly as possible.

Look for a doorway, an alley, a side street, or a safe building in which to get shelter. If possible, find a safe enclosed area. Riots often occur on the streets, making it necessary for a building to offer some protection. Stay away from doors and windows and try to find sheltered rooms. Make a note of all the exits in case you must leave in a hurry. Once the crowd has passed, leave moving in the opposite direction. Do your best to stay informed as events unfold. Social media may provide rapid coverage of events, but keep in mind that it can be less accurate than established media sources. Try to access as many resources as possible. Although civil unrest is by nature unpredictable, staying calm and monitoring the situation are key to keeping yourself and your loved ones safe in high-risk situations.

Notes on Public Health Emergencies: Having just lived through a global pandemic of epic proportions, we should pause and make sure we have absorbed the lessons. A public health emergency is defined as "an occurrence or imminent threat of an illness or health condition, caused by bio terrorism, epidemic or pandemic disease, or an infectious agent or biological toxin, that poses a substantial risk to humans by either causing a significant number of human fatalities or permanent or long-term disability." Public health emergencies also include influenza, or "the Flu." How you should react to a public health emergency depends on the emergency itself. Every situation is different, and different factors will impact the decisions made by officials. The skills and knowledge we acquired during the COVID-19 era will largely be beneficial. Discuss potential vaccines (such as the flu vaccine) with your healthcare provider. Washing your hands frequently is always a good idea. Make sure to cover coughs and sneezes with tissues while avoiding close contact with people who are sick. Be sure to avoid touching your eyes, nose, and mouth. And most importantly, if you are ill, avoid others and stay home.

Your Turn: Assess the top five human-caused hazard risks in your area on your own. Include any and everything safety-related that concerns you. Include human-caused emergencies. Then, consult a professionally prepared risk assessment of where you live. Consider using the United States National Risk Index below if appropriate for you. How did they match? Remember, just like before, your assessment is not "wrong" if different. It is your own perception, which is fine. If large hazardous material spills concern you, make them part of your planning. However, such incidents are generally not part of regional risk assessments, so you will need to consult other resources specific to these hazards. Write down your "Top Five" human-caused emergencies for planning purposes on the worksheet.

Pro Tip: Ask your local fire department or emergency medical services what THEY think are the most significant human-caused hazards in your area. They will be happy to talk to you, and you will be very surprised to hear their perspective. These issues will be based on known risks, not just the history of events.

Resources for Day 16: Human-Caused Disasters

United States National Risk Index

https://hazards.fema.gov/nri/

U.S. Centers for Disease Control Chemical Emergency Preparedness

https://www.cdc.gov/chemical-emergencies/response/index.html

U.S. Red Cross Chemical Emergency Preparedness

https://www.redcross.org/get-help/how-to-prepare-for-emergencies/types-of-emergencies/chemical-emergency.html

U.S. Department of Labor Occupational Safety and Health Administration (scroll down to oil, chemical, biological, radiological, nuclear, and explosive – CBRNE incidents)

https://www.osha.gov/emergency-preparedness

Harvard Global Support Services (for international travel)

https://www.globalsupport.harvard.edu/travel/advice/civil-unrest-planning

Florida State University Civil Unrest Guidance

https://emergency.fsu.edu/hazards/civil-unrest

U.S. Centers for Disease Control Office of Readiness and Response / Public Health Emergencies

https://www.cdc.gov/orr/index.html

National Association of County and City Health Officials (NACCHO) Public Health Preparedness

https://www.naccho.org/programs/public-health-preparedness

Notes

_____

_____

_____

_____

_____

_____

_____

_____

_____

Day 17
Let There Be Light (and Power)

"Let There Be Light."

– John 1 Genesis 1

In the Bible, we learn that God said, "Let there be light," and from there, a divine act of speech introduces a new day of creation, and light itself came into being. Imagine a world without light? In Day 16, we addressed human-caused emergencies, including a long-term power outage, which warrants its own day due to the significance of electricity in modern life. Most people experience a power outage as a minor inconvenience lasting a few minutes or up to a couple of hours during a storm. Sudden power outages can be frustrating and troublesome, especially when they last a long time. Although the news has discussed cyber-attacks as a source of power loss for several years, numerous potential points of failure exist throughout distribution, transmission, and storage networks for power. Modern electrical grids are more vulnerable than we think.

The wrong driver hitting the wrong transformer can bring down regional power. If a power outage is two hours or less, you need not be concerned about losing your perishable foods. For prolonged power outages, though, there are steps you can take to minimize food loss and to keep all members of your household as comfortable as possible. To help preserve your food, keep a few things handy like inexpensive Styrofoam coolers, ice, and a digital thermometer.

Surrounding food with ice in a cooler or in the refrigerator will keep food colder for a longer period during a prolonged power outage. A digital thermometer can quickly check the internal temperatures of food to ensure they are cold enough to be used safely. If your food thaws, cook it before it goes terrible. Beyond food, take an inventory now of the items you need that rely on electricity. Talk to your medical provider about a power outage plan for medical devices powered by electricity and refrigerated medicines. Find out how long medication can be stored at higher temperatures and get specific guidance for any medications that are critical for life. Think about your power supply without the grid and plan for batteries and other alternatives to meet your needs when the power goes out. As we mentioned earlier, sign up for local alerts and warning systems and monitor weather reports because strong summer and winter storm systems can cause power outages. This is where the weather radio comes in very handy! Determine now whether your home phone will work in a power outage and how long the battery backup will last. Have flashlights with extra batteries for every household member and in each room of your home, while also having enough nonperishable food and water. Use a thermometer in the refrigerator and freezer so that you can know the temperature when the power is restored. Keep mobile phones, other electronic equipment, and gas tanks charged. Full. Plan for weather extremes that might combine with this power outage, as losing power on a clear spring day is one thing, but it can become life-threatening in extreme heat and cold.

Your Turn: Assess your power needs. Write down your major power- use items and develop backup plans or alternative sources of power for them. How can you charge things without power? Maybe solar panels or different types of batteries make sense. Battery- powered cellular phone chargers are a great, inexpensive item to have in multiple locations. For some people, given the frequency and severity of power outages, a home generator could make sense. Scaling down from that, a smaller power generator just for a few appliances might do the trick. Remember always to check the safety precautions on any generator you use.

Pro Tip: Stage a long-term power outage drill in your home by making sure you know how to shut off your home or apartment's power. If shutting down the power is not possible, keep the lights off and unplug appliances. This could be "announced" or "unannounced" for family members. This drill will test your plan. Keep electricity off for at least twenty-four hours. Do your backup plans work? Does the family know where the flashlights are in the home or apartment?

Resources for Day 17: Let There Be Light (and Power)

U.S. Centers for Disease Control: Keeping Food Safe After a Disaster or Emergency

https://www.cdc.gov/food-safety/foods/keep-food-safe-after-emergency.html

U.S. Red Cross Power Outage Preparedness

https://www.redcross.org/get-help/how-to-prepare-for-emergencies/types-of-emergencies/power-outage.html.

Energy Harbor Power Outage Emergency Kit

https://energyharbor.com/en/energy-resources/moving-center/power-outage-emergency-kit-checklist-guide

Notes

Day 18
Cyber Preparedness

Effective cybersecurity is not a product, but a process.

–Jim Langevin

Cybersecurity is part of our everyday life. During a disaster or emergency, the situation becomes even more critical due to the presence of a large number of miscreants who are waiting to take advantage of vulnerable people in and around the crisis. Hackers and scammers are just waiting to take advantage of you during your weakest moments. We need to incorporate cybersecurity into our overall emergency planning more effectively. A little preparation in this area can go a long way in keeping you safe. As technology is continuously evolving, so are the threats that target our digital assets. Proper cybersecurity and encryption software are more important than ever before. In addition to the activities we completed on Day 5 to create a virtual or digital go bag, perform these steps routinely before an emergency or disaster to ensure your and your family's safety. Keep software and operating systems up to date. Use strong passwords and two-factor authentication, and watch for suspicious activity. This could be any message that asks you to complete a task immediately, offers something that seems too good to be true, or asks for personal information related to disaster recovery or emergency assistance. Use encrypted (secure) internet communications. Utilize antivirus and firewall solutions to block malware and other threats, and regularly back up your files to an encrypted file or storage device. Limit the personal information you share online, adjust your privacy settings, and deactivate location features. Protect your home network by changing the administrative and Wi-Fi passwords regularly.

Your Turn: Assess your own cybersecurity posture. How many of the things above do you do on a routine basis? An emergency will not wait for you to get ready. Do this now.

Pro Tip: Follow the "Shields Up" Guidance from the U.S. Critical Infrastructure Security Agency (CISA). Apply this to families, organizations, and businesses, as applicable to your situation. Actual preparedness starts at the individual level and then builds through organizations.

https://www.cisa.gov/shields-up

Resources for Day 18: Cyber Preparedness

The U.S. Critical Infrastructure Security Agency (CISA) offers a range of valuable guidance and assistance programs.

https://www.cisa.gov/

The U.S. Federal Emergency Management Agency (FEMA) provides numerous valuable tips and resources on this topic.

https://www.ready.gov/cybersecurity

Teckpert explains how to integrate cybersecurity into emergency preparedness.

https://www.teckpert.com/news/incorporating-cybersecurity-into-emergency-preparedness-programs

If cybersecurity is entirely new for you, you may find free training through the Texas A&M School of Engineering Cyber Readiness Center.

https://teex.org/program/cybersecurity/

Notes

Day 19
Thoughts on First Aid

Every single person in the world has the capacity to save a life. It is an essential gesture of solidarity. First aid education should be accessible to all without discrimination.

–Grace Lo

There are dozens of excellent books and courses accessible to you about first aid. First aid is fun! When did you last take a first aid course? They are all worthwhile and provide you with a wealth of knowledge about how the human body works and physical anatomy. First aid refers to the initial medical attention given immediately after a n injury or an accident. It is a short-term treatment that does not require special training or technology to administer, but is vital because it helps one be the first link in the chain of survival. However, having said that, have you ever reflected on the content of the courses you took? Most local community first aid training focuses on pain management and transporting the injured to a higher level of care. In a gesture of full confession, as a Scout many years ago, I struggled with tying the ankle bandage correctly, which was my last requirement on the First Aid Merit Badge. Eventually, I got it! Keeping with the same preparedness themes we have been discussing, you are, and always have been, your own first responder. Plan accordingly. This is not meant to be some kind of trite and stoic catch phrase.

The idea is that we are responsible for ourselves in times of emergency, as those charged with responding to crises (such as fire, criminal act, or natural hazard) will be exceedingly busy. So busy in fact, that barring the threat to life, limb, property, or the environment, they may not be able to get to you for days. This is the practical reason for a three-day go-bag and why each of your emergency kits for evacuation, vehicle, home, and office should have a first aid kit. You are the first link in the chain of survival for yourself, your co-workers, and your family. Nobody is expecting you to have the skills of a law enforcement officer, firefighter, or emergency medical technician; however, there are some practical skills that we can master that save lives. Some of these skills fall into the first aid category. When addressing first aid knowledge, focus on the areas of preventable death, i.e., things that will kill you in less than five minutes. We are buying time for medical professionals to arrive. Nobody will die from a broken arm or twisted ankle. However, people will die from massive hemorrhaging (excessive bleeding), obstructed airways, hypothermic reaction to trauma known as shock, and tension pneumothorax (compromise of the chest wall and lungs that prevents breathing properly, which can be a hole going in and perhaps also coming out). If we, as laypeople, can fix these things quickly, we save lives. First aid training does not have to cost a lot of money. Look in your community for those providing it; often, it is free. If your community lacks personnel, time, and other resources to conduct first aid training, empower yourself to be the key leader who helps get it started again by volunteering to help set it up and attend. Becoming an instructor in various areas is not that taxing.

Nevertheless, do not wait for organizationally sponsored training because an emergency will not wait until you are trained. Think big but start small. To that end, did you know you could learn and practice many of these individual skills online?

Fantastic courses like "Stop the Bleed," "Until Help Arrives," "Revive!," and many others are available right now. In addition to honing your basic first aid skills, we should all enhance our community support. Everyone is a leader, and everyone is a first responder. Do you believe this? Do you have this mindset? We must act toward this goal through repetitive training and education that challenges us to learn and practice basic first aid skills. At work or while shopping, as you walk past the Automated External Defibrillators (AEDs) in the hallway, do you know how to use them? AEDs can significantly increase a cardiac arrest victim's chance of survival. Relatedly, cardiopulmonary resuscitation (CPR) is an emergency lifesaving procedure performed when the heart stops beating. Immediate CPR can double and even triple a colleague's chance of survival when performed correctly and quickly. Survival and safety are all about initiative and the desire for all of us to learn more before an emergency. During a crisis, first responders will be extremely busy, and we may have to save ourselves, our families, or our colleagues. Do you know what to do? Train today so that you and others may live tomorrow.

Your Turn: Confirm you have usable first aid kits in your home, vehicle, and office. Many first aid kits have not been opened in years. Inspect the contents. Using the basic list of needed supplies, make, purchase, or upgrade as necessary.

Pro Tip: Utilize the helpful links below or other community resources to create a personalized first aid training plan, incorporating Stop the Bleed, Until Help Arrives, and a Basic First Aid Course.

Resources for Day 19: Thoughts on First Aid

First Aid Kits are easy to make on your own with the basic lists. Some helpful suggestions on what to add may be found with these resources.

American Red Cross First Aid Kit

https://www.redcross.org/get-help/how-to-prepare-for-emergencies/anatomy-of-a-first-aid-kit.html

Mayo Clinic First Aid Kits

https://www.mayoclinic.org/first-aid/first-aid-kits/basics/art-20056673

Brown University Health

https://www.brownhealth.org/lifespan-living/12-key-items-first-aid-kits

Stop the Bleed is a U.S. national initiative developed after the Boston bombing in 2013 to get more people trained and ready to stop victims from bleeding to death. Courses and many resources are available for free. Search "Stop the Bleed" and you will find many resources.

https://www.stopthebleed.org/

https://www.dhs.gov/stopthebleed

Until Help Arrives expands on Stop the Bleed. This course explains what to do for all kinds of emergencies and how to be the first link in the chain of survival. While a skills session is recommended after this online course, feel free to get started now because emergencies can happen fast. As we mentioned previously, emergency responders are not always nearby. You may be able to save a life by taking simple actions immediately. The webinar links below were from four separate sessions conducted during 2021 with different instructors, but the course is the same.

https://fema.connectsolutions.com/pjpdz6wrldqn/

https://fema.connectsolutions.com/p2c9sm2f7l43/

https://fema.connectsolutions.com/pxvrtbbijwvb/

https://fema.connectsolutions.com/pfymf5c4f0ln/

If a pre-recorded webinar isn't your learning style, consider taking the course online in a more formal setting by searching for "Until Help Arrives," which offers updates from several organizations. The U.S. Department of Homeland Security (DHS) version offers a certificate of completion for finishing the course. Take the first step and resolve to improve your individual level of preparedness soon because your family and the organizations you belong to depend on you knowing what to do in case of an emergency and having the skills to act.

AED and CPR for Free are as advertised: quick, user-friendly training available online for free. You do not have to register, but if you do, the system keeps track of your progress, and you can earn multiple certifications that include CPR, AED, Adult and Pediatric First Aid, Bloodborne Pathogens, and more. These classes (with slight variation) and more can also be found at First Aid for Free, which offers basic and advanced first aid, CPR, AED, Pediatric First Aid, and Anaphylaxis Awareness and Asthma Awareness. Registering is free and allows one to download certifications, manuals, and other resources.

AED and CPR for Free

https://www.aedcpr.com/free-classes/

First Aid for Free

https://www.firstaidforfree.com/

Learn from the best. The U.S. Army Tactical Combat Casualty Care (TCCC) manual is available for free as a download.

https://api.army.mil/e2/c/downloads/2023/01/19/31e03488/ 17-13-tactical-casualty-combat-care-handbook-v5-may-17-distro-a.pdf

Notes

_____

_____

_____

_____

_____

_____

_____

_____

Day 20
Financial First Aid

*Money is better than **poverty**, if only for financial reasons.*

−Woody Allen

A disaster or emergency is one of life's most significant challenges. Financial first aid will be a lifeline for economic well-being and recovery. Do not let unexpected emergencies derail you! Reclaim control, ditch the stress, and build a solid plan for whatever comes next. Crises can cause anyone to snap into panic mode, especially if their home or business is destroyed. But instead of falling into fear, we need to ensure we have a game plan so that financial stability is always on standby. Now, we need to build your financial first aid kit to navigate financial setbacks.

What are your insurance needs? Ensure your home, auto, or renters' insurance coverage is up to date. Also, make sure all relevant information is included in your Virtual or Digital Go Bag from Day 5. Nobody owes you the replacement value of anything unless it is well documented. If you do not have flood insurance and do not think you need it, ask a qualified consultant. While your community may not have a history of flooding, localized conditions could make isolated flooding a possibility. Reconsider your risks from Day 7.

It is critical to build an emergency fund in case of unexpected, costly difficulties. This fund should include at least three to six months' worth of living expenses to help hold you over if you lose your source of income and encounter sizable expenses at the same time. Without an emergency fund, many people resort to high-interest credit cards or loans, which can spiral into long-term debt. A well-funded safety net provides stability, flexibility, reduces financial stress, and allows you to focus on solutions and rebuilding instead of scrambling to cover immediate costs. If your community is devastated, local, state, federal governments, and NGOs will respond with immediate assistance for food, water, clothing, and shelter. Still, these are temporary solutions until the community infrastructure starts working again. And while this is all very helpful, none of them is permanent. Individuals are expected to take care of themselves at some point. The better prepared financially you are, the easier this will be. This is your responsibility and not the government's.

Once a major emergency strikes, the first priority is to assess the damage holistically and determine the financial impact. How much do you need, and how soon do you need to have those funds? Next, check your bank accounts, emergency funds, and any immediate sources of relief (side jobs, savings, or family support), then organize your action plan. Consider exploring additional income streams, such as joining the gig economy or selling used items. It is time to streamline and prioritize essential expenses. You will want to limit spending to your core essentials. Focus on covering the basics such as shelter, utilities, food, transportation, and any necessary insurance. If you do not already have a budget, now is the time to list all your expenses and separate needs from wants. Moving forward, your budget is your best friend and guide to staying financially on track and prepared for emergencies. Unnecessary expenses, such as subscriptions, dining out, and impulse buying, can wait until you are on solid footing after the disaster. Do not ignore the bills you cannot pay! Contact creditors and service providers. Always communicate. Additional measures can be taken to reduce expenses further and protect your credit, especially if there is an official disaster declaration in your area. Many lenders, utility companies, and landlords offer hardship programs, payment extensions, or reduced payments during financial distress. Call them, explain your situation, and ask about your options before you fall behind.

There are many resources designed to help during disasters and emergencies. Explore local and national assistance programs for personal and business finances. Depending on your situation, you may qualify for a range of programs. Short-term loans can offer quick relief without the hassle of a credit check or the risk of non-bank payday lenders. Unemployment benefits help temporarily bridge the financial gap while you search for a new job or rebuild your home. Do not be too proud to accept assistance. Apply as soon as possible, as demand is expected to be high in your area. Consider local or national government aid, such as food and utility assistance.

Once the emergency or disaster has stabilized, protect your financial future by taking proactive steps to prevent the next one. Start or rebuild your emergency fund. Consider insurance coverage for medical, auto, or home issues based on your recent experience. Do you need an update? This will prevent future financial stress. Prioritize best financial practices, such as living below your means and regularly investing whenever you have an excess of income.

By working on these tasks consistently, you are shaping up to build financial stability, not just for emergencies but in life overall. Weathering hardships is much easier when you plan and make positive money habits. Do not let a setback define your financial future; use it as motivation to improve your financial wellness.

Your Turn: Review all your financial assets and resources and put them on a document or spreadsheet. Determine your current savings and cash flow. Do you have three months' savings set aside? Are all your valuables insured, especially your home and vehicle? Is it enough?

Pro Tip: Emergency preparedness in the private sector is often called "business continuity." If you own a business, consider doing the planning above, but focus on getting your business up and running as quickly as possible after a disaster. According to the U.S. Federal Emergency Management Agency (FEMA), forty percent of companies do not reopen after a disaster, and another twenty-five percent fail within one year. Fortunately, you can take proactive steps to mitigate the impact of a disaster on your business with the tools below.

Resources for Day 20: Financial First Aid

Fillable emergency financial first aid kits are available from the U.S. Federal Emergency Management Agency (FEMA) in multiple languages.

https://www.fema.gov/emergency-financial-first-aid-kit

Let the American Red Cross help your business or organization get ready by using the Ready Rating Program.

https://www.readyrating.org/

The American Red Cross also has business continuity planning tips.

https://www.redcross.org/take-a-class/resources/articles/business-continuity-planning-tips

FEMA offers free business continuity information, manuals, and videos.

https://www.ready.gov/business/emergency-plans/continuity-planning

Notes

Day 21
Cognitive Bias and Psychological First Aid

In the beginning, it is very painful; the wound is fresh. But by allowing people to talk about their experience, we try to turn it into a scar.

–Dr. Rashar Ghassan

The topics of cognitive bias, psychological first aid, emotional well-being, and disaster mental health can be infinitely complicated. I intend to give you a few things to consider for your own psychological preparedness, so you can better serve others. First, well before any emergency, we are predisposed psychologically as part of the human condition not always to make the right or rational decision. Cognitive biases take practice to work through because, in stressful situations, we may not realize they are influencing our minds. While there are dozens of key concepts to understand, we can address some of the important ones as they pertain to disaster preparedness and response.

Action Bias is when we prefer doing something to doing nothing. If you are sheltering in place because of an active shooter in your area, but you feel a pressing need to get something from your car, this bias could squarely put you in harm's way.

Anchoring Bias occurs when we compare everything to the first information we receive, even though this information is rarely accurate.

The Bandwagon Effect is why we support opinions as they become more popular. A group of neighbors deciding how to evacuate f r o m a wildfire may side with the most vocal or convincing person based on no actual information available.

Choice Overload occurs when we struggle to decide due to having too many options. If someone knows five ways to leave a burning building, they may become paralyzed with indecision.

Decision Fatigue occurs when our decision-making abilities suffer due to stress, tiredness, hunger, thirst, and other factors. Making decisions after not sleeping for two days rarely turns out well.

The Dunning-Kruger Effect is when we fail to gauge our own abilities accurately. This has a higher propensity in younger males. Sorry guys!

Fundamental Attribution Effect is when we underestimate the influence of the situation on people's behavior. During an emergency, all bets are off on how people will react.

The Hot Hand Fallacy occurs when we expect previous success to lead to future success. This explains why many people do not evacuate from a hurricane if they have survived a previous one without doing so.

Illusion of Control is the phenomenon where we believe we have more control over the world than we do. This can be a crushing weight on everyone after a disaster.

Normalcy Bias is when we believe nothing bad is going to happen. This is a particularly deadly bias in all emergency planning.

The Ostrich Effect refers to the tendency to ignore negative information. This bias combines with the **Optimism Bias,** which is when we overestimate the probability of success. A great example would be not to leave rising flood waters because the groups preparing the sandbags are doing a good job and have stopped the river before. And there are many, many more. I encourage you to read and study more about it on your own. The key point is that an unprepared mind struggles in an emergency. The more you can work through and examine your decision-making, the more successful you will be. The phrase "two heads are better than one" comes into play when another person can help you think through options and decisions, which can help eliminate your natural tendencies. Once we have a better grasp of our minds and how they work, we can be better prepared to help others.

It is always interesting to me how most people have a certain willingness to learn physical first aid, but will almost immediately eschew psychological first aid as only the purview of trained professionals, doctors, and counselors. Just like in regular first aid, we can be the help until help arrives through psychological first aid, or PFA. PFA can help lessen harm and speed recovery from traumatic events because it is an evidence-informed approach that is built on the concept of human resilience. PFA aims to reduce stress symptoms and assist in a healthy recovery following a traumatic event, natural disaster, public health emergency, or even a personal crisis. We can all learn it. Emotional distress is not always as visible as a physical injury, but it is just as painful and debilitating. After going through a life-altering experience, it is common to be affected emotionally. Everybody who experiences a disaster is touched by it. Reactions manifest differently at different periods during and after the incident. Some common stress reactions include confusion, fear, feelings of hopelessness and helplessness, sleep problems, physical pain, anxiety, anger, grief, aggressiveness, withdrawal, guilt, shaken religious faith, and loss of confidence. While physical first aid is used to reduce physical discomfort due to a bodily injury, PFA is a strategy to reduce the painful range of emotions and responses experienced by people exposed to high stress. There are many courses and principles written about PFA, but essentially, we need to prepare, look or observe, listen, and link. These actions can also apply to self-care for first responders and others who are helping people in stressful situations.

Your Turn: Plan to become more familiar with Psychological First Aid over time, either through reading some of the material below or taking a course. Set a date to accomplish this goal within the next sixty days.

Pro Tip: Understanding yourself, your decision-making, and self-care are essential during periods of high stress. From the learning during "Your Turn" above or other resources, learn how to calm yourself, reduce anxiety, and maximize decision outcomes. Just like in oxygen mask instructions on airplanes, we must learn to help ourselves before we help others. Other sources worth investigating include Mental Health First Aid, Disaster Mental Health, and Critical Incident Stress Management.

Resources for Day 21: Cognitive Bias and Psychological First Aid (PFA)

PFA training is abundant. One of the U.S. national standards on this course is free from the National Child Traumatic Stress Network (NCTSN).

https://learn.nctsn.org/course/index.php?categoryid=11

Download the NCTSN manual for free here.

https://www.nctsn.org/sites/default/files/resources/pfa_field_operations_guide.pdf

The Red Cross and Red Crescent Societies' short introduction to the PFA manual is a great resource.

https://pscentre.org/wp-content/uploads/2019/07/PFA-Intro-low.pdf

Free course offered by Johns Hopkins University on the Coursera platform.

https://www.coursera.org/learn/psychological-first-aid

Notes

_____

_____

_____

_____

_____

_____

_____

_____

Day 22
Disaster Fitness

It is not the strongest of the species that survives, nor the most intelligent that survives. It is the one that is the most adaptable to change.

–Charles Darwin

How fit are you? What is your current percentage of body fat? This is not an exercise or fat-shaming section of the book. The truth is that disasters and emergencies are very unkind to those out of shape and overweight. At the most difficult time of your life, you and your family will be under considerable stress. One should expect physical exertion, walking long distances, carrying things if you cannot evacuate by car, running short distances, lifting, digging, crawling, getting over obstacles, and much more. Can your heart and body take this? Take the time now to talk to your doctor and schedule your annual physical if you have not already done so for the year. You need to know your current level of fitness. It will be different from what it was in the past.

Once you have completed your physical and received permission to do so with a doctor's approval, complete the following "Disaster Physical Fitness Test" as directed, as one series of events conducted sequentially. Be sure to stretch properly before and after this activity while also hydrating appropriately. Equipment needed: a place to walk, a 25 lb. weight or equivalent, a comfortable flat piece of ground, a mat, a chair, an open space, a pull-up bar, or a tree branch.

1. Walk one mile at a brisk pace. (rest for five minutes and cool off)
2. Do ten pushups. (rest one minute)
3. Do twenty-five jumping jacks. (rest one minute)
4. Lift twenty-five lbs. above your head ten times. (rest one minute)
5. Lie flat on the ground on your stomach and get up in any way that is comfortable for you. Come to a full standing position. You do not need to move quickly through this. Do this ten times. (rest one minute)
6. Take an average chair and stand up on it with one leg to the full erect position (assist yourself by holding on to something if needed, making sure you have enough space to stand up fully erect). Do this five times with each leg. (rest one minute)
7. Using a pull-up bar or tree limb, simply hang for one minute with your feet off the ground. (rest one minute)
8. On a street or in a park, measure approximately fifty feet. Sprint to the end and sprint back, repeating this five times with thirty seconds of rest intervals in between. (rest one minute when all are complete)
9. On all fours (knees and hands), crawl thirty feet across a yard or park, then crawl back to the starting position. (rest one minute)
10. Find a table and get under it in any way you are able and sit or lie down for three minutes.

How do you feel? Was any of this difficult? These are the absolute minimum physical things you should be able to do to survive a disaster. If you don't already have a physical fitness habit, now is the time to establish one. Everyone should incorporate activities that promote their cardiovascular health, strength, mobility, and flexibility. Please consult your physician and physical fitness experts at your local gym to see what is best for your situation because your survival and overall health depend on it.

Your Turn: Based on the physical fitness test you just took, plan for improvement with an exercise professional or medical specialist. Place your physical activity plans on a calendar so they become part of your overall preparedness program.

Pro Tip: Have an honest conversation with yourself about your weight. Do you need to lose a few pounds? If so, consider healthy and steady alternatives to drugs, injections, or faddish diets. Focus on lifestyle and nutrition.

Resources for Day 22: Disaster Fitness

Mayo Clinic Fitness Basics

https://www.mayoclinic.org/healthy-lifestyle/fitness/basics/fitness-basics/hlv-20049447

American Heart Association Recommendations for Adults and Kids

https://www.heart.org/en/healthy-living/fitness/fitness-basics/aha-recs-for-physical-activity-in-adults

The Fiton app or website is free for basic access after signing up. There are hundreds of different kinds of workouts for different goals.

https://fitonapp.com/

Notes

Day 23
Building Resilience

Resilience is accepting your new reality, even if it is less good than the one you had before. You can fight it, you can do nothing but scream about what you have lost, or you can accept that and try to put together something that is good.

—Elizabeth Edwards

All of us have a "resilience battery," and it is either full, partially charged, or maybe even on empty. The term "resilience" means a lot of different things depending on the context. It is a term like "strategy" that has become overused. For our purposes, let us agree that resilience is our capacity to withstand or to recover quickly from difficulties. It implies toughness and bouncing back, or perhaps a certain emotional and physical elasticity. Maintaining healthy physical habits, such as getting enough sleep, eating well, managing stress, and limiting alcohol use, helps keep our resilience battery mostly charged. However, I have mentioned it several times in this book, each day of this program, you have been building your resilience or capacity to confront emergencies and disasters. Knowledge is power, as it reduces anxiety and fear about the unknown. On Day 22, Disaster Fitness, we began to assess our physical capabilities in the face of prolonged disasters, which could potentially lead to significant dislocation and discomfort. Nobody likes to be uncomfortable, but a little practice in this area goes a long way. Are there things in your life that naturally build physical, mental, and emotional stamina? If so, that is great. If not, consider incorporating activities that can help develop your capacities in this area.

In Day 1, Plan to Make a Plan, we discussed having the right attitude. Your positive outlook will help you survive, manage stress, and be a beacon of hope for those around you. While today might be the worst day of your life, we need to make tomorrow better for ourselves and those we care about. Positive people are tough people. How tough are you? Weak people make excuses because they're free. Look for ways to build mental and physical toughness by pushing yourself beyond your comfort zone. One way to achieve this is through periodic, purposeful activities that intentionally challenge comfort levels. Try a "resilience jar" by putting the following items on notecards and putting all the cards in a jar. Once a month, you randomly select a card and complete the associated activity as soon as possible. If the challenge is seasonal, pick another card that fits. Some challenges include, but are not limited to, the following:

1. Go swimming in a gym or pool. Swim actively for at least thirty minutes. Remember Day 12 Water Safety, you may have to swim when you least expect it.

2. Next time it rains, go for a walk with appropriate rain gear. Avoid lightning. In a disaster, you may have to walk in the rain. Does your gear work?

3. When safe to do so, go for a long walk in new snow or while it is still snowing. Does your gear work?

4. Try a new sport. Emergencies and disasters prompt us to respond in different ways.

5. Take an ice bath or cold shower. If you evacuate to a shelter, they

may not have hot water.

6. Take a sauna (dry or wet). In our air-conditioned world, our bodies have become accustomed to not being hot.

7. Go to a park or forest and sit next to a tree without looking at your phone for thirty minutes, and close your eyes. What sounds do you hear? Slowing down your mind and being present is an important skill.

8. Go camping overnight. Cooking outside and sleeping on the ground in a sleeping bag could be your lot in life if you cannot return to the inside of your home for a while. Test all your gear. Can you live outside for three days?

9. Go for a hike (more than three miles) on designated trails in a park or forest. Walking on uneven ground helps build our feet, which will help prevent blistering if we are called upon to walk long distances.

10. In an area safe to do so and with permission, hike over open terrain from one point to another. Were there any obstacles like fences or creeks? What did you do about them? We may have to take unknown routes during disasters.

11. Start your day at 3:00 am. Try to have a normal workday. Occasionally, pushing the boundaries of sleep can increase our tolerance of sleep deprivation if necessary.

12. Without using your GPS, drive to another town near you to a designated location and back. Using maps is a lost art. Have maps handy and use your GPS less. You may not have access to a GPS in an emergency.

These are just a few things you could do to build your

resilience. What else could you include? Pick things relevant to you. Every Superman has their kryptonite! List things you dislike or are fearful of, and they'll boost your resilience battery. Lastly, if you suffer from addictions of any kind, they will only be exacerbated during periods of crisis. Address these now so you do not have to face them in the middle of what could be the most difficult moments of your life.

Your Turn: Build your resilience jar with the tasks above and some of your own. Start now. Do a task as soon as you can. Throughout your day, look for small things that can make you more resilient. Take the stairs where you live or work. Park farther away to go grocery shopping.

Pro Tip: Help those you love and work with to be more resilient by involving them in the tasks and program ideas above. Make it fun and challenging for the whole group! How about one of those mud races? A deep-sea fishing trip? Escape room? Anything that brings the group together to do new things, incorporating at least a small element of physical activity and/or discomfort, helps build resilience.

Resources for Day 23: Building Resilience

American Psychological Association – Building Resilience

https://www.apa.org/topics/resilience/building-your-resilience

Mayo Clinic – Build Skills to Endure Hardship

https://www.mayoclinic.org/tests-procedures/resilience-training/in-depth/resilience/art-20046311

Harvard Business Review – Building Resilience

https://hbr.org/2011/04/building-resilience

Notes

_____

_____

_____

_____

_____

_____

_____

_____

_____

_____

_____

_____

_____

_____

_____

_____

Day 24
Emergency Planning for
Unique Circumstances

Disabilities can impact a person in a variety of ways— both visible and invisible. For people with disabilities and their families, it is important to consider individual circumstances and needs to effectively prepare for emergencies and disasters.

–U.S. Federal Emergency Management Agency (FEMA)

Let's talk for a moment about differing abilities. How did you do with the Disaster Fitness Test on Day 22? Do you have problems getting up and down? Do things hurt too much in specific ranges of movement or in joints? Even if this is temporary due to recent surgery or other circumstances, you might have what is known as an "Access or Functional Need" (AFN). AFN refers to individuals with and without disabilities, who may need additional assistance because of any condition that may limit their ability to act in an emergency. Although temporary, pregnant women would fit here and are a great example of many people who can move in and out of this category. Everything we have discussed thus far in this book applies, such as making plans on Day 1 and building our various kits and risks in Days 2 – 7. What one must do is examine one's own and one's family's unique circumstances and see what else needs to be done. Possible needs for AFN consideration include, but are not limited to, the deaf or hard of hearing, low vision or blind, intellectual impairment, communication difficulties, Alzheimer's and related dementia, mobility disabilities, and those whose primary language is not the language of local emergency communication for alerts and warnings. Disability intersects every demographic group, and there are people with disabilities of all ages, races, sexes, and national origins. Your additional planning in this area saves lives and reduces stress for those with extra challenges during emergencies. I have included lots of unique circumstance resources below.

Other emergency planning unique circumstances include older adults, children, and pets. As an older adult, you may be living on your own and have specific needs after a disaster. Use the information in the guide below to assess your needs and take simple, low-cost steps that help you get better prepared. Do you know an older person? Check in on them and make sure the appropriate plans are in place. Children are not just small adults, and they have unique planning and emotional needs from infants to teens. Sadly, children are no longer being taught emergency preparedness or first aid skills at school, or, more importantly, at home. Interestingly, children make up a significant portion of the human population on the planet. Yet, despite this vulnerability, scant attention has been given to this population regarding emergency preparedness and planning. We often overlook children's needs and experiences during disasters, as well as their role in disaster preparedness education and training. Fortunately, generations of lost knowledge can be quickly recovered by involving kids of all ages in simple activities. Everything we have done in this book is family-friendly. Now that you have more knowledge, involve the children in your life with every planning aspect of this program, from emergency planning to communication. Emergency preparedness brings many messages of hope and love, not doom and gloom.

Having kids help with their go-bags makes them vested in the process and the outcome. When doing any of these activities, remember to think like a child and try to make it fun! This doesn't have to be an uncomfortable or scary topic.

Plenty of games, puzzles, worksheets, coloring books, scavenger hunts, and other activities can be found online. Some games sponsored by the United States Federal Emergency Management Agency (FEMA) include "Disaster Master," "Build a Kit Game," and "Ready 2 Help." Many campaigns include entire thematic systems of materials. FEMA's culturally inclusive initiative is "Prepare with Pedro," which replaced "Disaster Heroes" (which can still be found online). Another notable example is the United States Centers for Disease Control's "Ready Wrigley." Lastly, pets are important. We love our pets and want to protect them, too. As a matter of fact, a lot of research has gone into evacuation planning, and those who have not considered their pets in planning are more likely to risk their own lives over their pets' when faced with leaving them or not. So, we need to include them because having a plan in place for you and your pets will likely reduce the difficulty, stress, and worry you experience when making decisions during an emergency. If local officials ask you to evacuate, that means your pet should evacuate too. Plan, build a kit for your pet, and prepare pets for travel with the resources below.

Your Turn: Do a quick review of your situation and determine if any AFN concepts apply to you in this program. Put a date on the calendar within the next thirty days to address each circumstance.

Pro Tip: For any emergency planning circumstance identified in "Your Turn" above, train for and conduct a drill to implement the solution. For example, if your grandfather lives thirty minutes away and uses a walker for mobility assistance, practice and drill your evacuation plan with and for him. Another example could be to practice an evacuation with your pet. Does your pet have a go bag? Do you have a copy of all vaccinations? Do you have the appropriate carrier?

Resources for Day 24: Emergency Planning Unique for Circumstances

Access and Functional Needs (AFN)

U.S. Federal Emergency Management Agency (FEMA) Disabilities Page

https://www.ready.gov/people-disabilities

MEMA Webinar on Inclusive Emergency Management

https://www.youtube.com/watch?v=Hs6-0-v3IqI

U.S. Department of Health and Human Services (HHS) Administration for Strategic Preparedness and Response (ASPR) AFN

https://aspr.hhs.gov/at-risk/Pages/at-risk_afn.aspx

U.S. Centers for Disease Control (CDC) Emergency Preparedness and Disability Inclusion

https://www.cdc.gov/disability-emergency-preparedness/resources/index.html

CDC AFN Toolkit

https://www.cdc.gov/readiness/media/pdfs/CDC_Access_and_Functional_Needs_Toolkit_March2021.pdf

U.S. Institutes of Health Planning for Special Needs

https://ors.od.nih.gov/ser/dem/emergencyPrep/Pages/Planning-for-Special-Needs.aspx

Considerations for Older Adults

U.S. Federal Emergency Management Agency (FEMA) Older Adult Page

https://www.ready.gov/older-adults

FEMA Disaster Preparedness Guide for Older Adults

https://www.ready.gov/sites/default/files/2023-09/ready-gov_disaster-preparedness-guide-for-older-adults.pdf

American Association of Retired Persons (AARP) Disaster Preparedness

https://www.aarp.org/home-family/your-home/disaster-preparedness.html

AARP Disaster Resilience Took Kit

https://www.aarp.org/livable-communities/tool-kits-resources/info-2022/aarp-disaster-resilience-tool-kit-download.html

Considerations for Children

American Red Cross – How Schools Can Prepare for Disasters

https://www.redcross.org/get-help/how-to-prepare-for-emergencies/emergency-preparedness-for-kids/school-disaster-preparedness.html

American Red Cross – Teaching Kids About Emergency Preparedness

https://www.redcross.org/get-help/how-to-prepare-for-emergencies/emergency-preparedness-for-kids.html

FEMA Ready Kids

https://www.ready.gov/kids

National Weather Service Just for Kids

https://www.weather.gov/cae/justforkids.html

Safe Kids Worldwide

https://www.safekids.org/

Considerations of Pets

American Red Cross Pet Preparedness

https://www.redcross.org/get-help/how-to-prepare-for-emergencies/pet-disaster-preparedness.html

FEMA Prepare Your Pets for Disasters

https://www.ready.gov/pets

American Veterinary Medical Association Pets and Disasters

https://www.avma.org/resources-tools/pet-owners/emergency-care/pets-and-disasters

American Society for the Prevention of Cruelty to Animals (ASPCA) Pet Disaster Preparedness

https://www.aspca.org/pet-care/general-pet-care/disaster-preparedness

CDC Build a Pet Disaster Preparedness Kit

https://www.cdc.gov/healthy-pets/emergency-preparedness/preparedness-kit.html

U.S. National Institutes of Health Caring for Animals

https://ors.od.nih.gov/ser/dem/emergencyPrep/Pages/Caring%20for%20Animals.aspx

Notes

_____

_____

_____

_____

_____

_____

_____

_____

_____

Day 25
Emergency Preparedness
on a Budget

A budget tells us what we can afford, but it doesn't keep us from buying it.

–William Feather

Emergency preparedness doesn't have to break the bank. As a matter of fact, you should not simply throw money into the problem because you cannot buy yourself readiness. It does nobody any good to have a garage full of expensive gear that you never touch or use and consider yourself "prepared." Disasters are costly, but preparing for them doesn't have to be. In fact, taking time to prepare now can help save you thousands of dollars and give you peace of mind when the next disaster or emergency occurs. Some estimates out there demonstrate that for every dollar we spend on preparedness, we save seven in response and recovery. Planning and being ready for an emergency are worthwhile investments that can fit into most budgets when done over time. Dollar stores, garage sales, thrift stores, and online marketplaces are great places to find items for many of the things we have discussed thus far. Take these simple steps now and start with the basics to be better prepared for any disaster or emergency that has little to no cost. You can use a plastic bin or a duffel bag to keep all your emergency supplies in one place. Begin with food and water, then gradually add other items as your budget allows. Dollar stores often carry a variety of non-perishable food items. Check the flyers and promotions at grocery stores and other retailers for sales on cases of water, canned, and other non-perishable foods. Before you go shopping, take a look around your home for items you are not using; they might be repurposed into "emergency duty." Phone chargers and cords come to mind. You might be surprised by what is lying around, not being used very often. Dig into your closets and drawers and pull out those rarely used pieces to add to your kit.

Try building a first aid kit using extra items you may already have, like bandages, sterile gauze pads, adhesive tape, antiseptic wipes or soap, tweezers, and scissors. Check out the list below from the American Red Cross to help you get started. I have been making first aid kits for different purposes all my life. When you make your own, you know exactly what is in there when you need it. For many small but necessary items, visit your local dollar or thrift store to stock up. You will likely be able to find garbage bags, foil blankets, rain ponchos, tarps, straps, tissue paper, rope, utility knives, whistles, can openers, wipes, and work gloves. Thrift stores can be another valuable resource for items like extra seasonal clothing, extra bags, or old backpacks. Keep an eye open for sales. Many locations have tax-free days when you can purchase emergency preparedness items. Look for good-quality batteries with a longer shelf life; this will save money over time. Alternatively, consider investing in rechargeable batteries that you can use more than once.

Remember, you do not need to buy new stuff if it works! In an emergency, you will need a reliable flashlight. Chances are you will be able to find one at a local thrift store or garage sale. You can also check your local online marketplace for used items that are sometimes free. A battery-powered or hand-crank radio is essential for getting timely updates during an emergency.

Your Turn: Based on the work you have done so far in this book, identify additional items that you may need for emergency preparedness. Before purchasing them new, consider seeking alternatives that are cheaper or even free. Work this into your monthly budget and buy the items you need within the next thirty days.

Pro Tip: Sometimes used or reduced-price items come in bulk, like a pack of six flashlights. One may think, "I don't need six." But become the person who regifts these items to friends and family on special occasions, demonstrating your care for them and their level of preparedness. Use this as a segue to deeper conversations about their emergency plans.

Resources for Day 25: Emergency Preparedness on a Budget

American Red Cross First Aid Kit List

https://www.redcross.org/get-help/how-to-prepare-for-emergencies/anatomy-of-a-first-aid-kit.html

Oregon Office of Emergency Management Budget-Friendly Emergency Preparedness

https://apps.oregon.gov/oregon-newsroom/OR/OEM/Posts/Post/Budget-Friendly-Emergency-Preparedness-Simple-Steps-To-Stay-Safe

Fairfax County, Virginia Division of Emergency Preparedness and Response Five Low-Cost Ways to Build Your Supplies Kit

https://www.fairfaxcounty.gov/health/emergency-preparedness-budget-5-low-cost-ways-build-supplies-kit

Notes

_____

_____

_____

_____

_____

_____

_____

_____

_____

_____

Day 26
Emergency Preparedness While Traveling

*So much of who **we** are is where we have been.*

—William Langewiesche

One of life's greatest pleasures is to unwind, travel somewhere different, and have new experiences. Many would consider travel as a time to forget about serious preoccupations and explore or relax. You should do all of that and more, but a little emergency preparedness, common sense, and following the principles you have learned thus far in this book will go a long way in keeping you and your loved ones safe. Just as we did earlier for where we live, know your destination's vulnerability to natural disasters (hurricanes, storm surges, earthquakes, flooding, wildfires, etc.) and be alert. Enable emergency alerts on your cell phone. Most cell carriers can issue alerts as you travel through the areas you are visiting. In addition, install the CodeRED mobile app to receive alerts from home. Upon arrival, please create an identification card for young children that includes the family name, hotel, phone number, your name, and cell phone number.

Use a safety pin to attach it to a piece of their clothing. If they wander off, someone will be able to identify them. If you have little children who don't know your name or cell phone number, consider writing it on their arm with a permanent marker. You can be creative with magic markers for short day trips. While I understand restrictions on weight, especially for flights, it's best to err on the side of caution. Pack a travel-size emergency supply kit with essentials like water, snacks, a first-aid kit, a flashlight, a small battery-operated radio, extra batteries, and an emergency contact card with names and phone numbers. Pack extra supplies of critical items, such as prescription medications and baby formula, in case your return is delayed. Make copies of all essential documents, including passports, prescriptions (with both generic and brand names for your medications), IDs, insurance cards, etc. Or you may want to consider a copy of your digital go bag we prepared on Day 5. Let family and friends know your itinerary and how to reach you. Using the concepts you completed in Day 6, develop a communications plan and make everyone in your traveling group aware of the plan. Do you know the address and number of where you are staying? Ensure everyone has the cell phone numbers of the others in your group. Designate an out-of-area person to contact in case your group is separated during an emergency and unable to place local calls.

Your Turn: Plan your next trip, keeping the emergency preparedness tips above in mind. If you don't have any scheduled trips, imagine a place you would like to visit. Run through every item above, take the time to gather the necessary items, and make plans. After doing this more than once, it will become second nature. Please do not travel without emergency planning.

Pro Tip: On your next trip, plan a travel drill or emergency exercise to walk through potential scenarios and test your plans and understanding. Here are some questions to get you started. What would we do if someone were in an accident? Who do we call in case of an emergency? If all flights are cancelled, what are the alternative ways of leaving? Based on your travel location, what are some of the more common natural hazards, and how could they affect you?

Resources for Day 26: Emergency Preparedness While Traveling

If traveling internationally, register with the U.S. Department of State through a free online service at the Smart Traveler Enrollment Program (STEP), which allows travelers to enter information about upcoming trips abroad so that the Department of State can better assist them in an emergency. Those registered will get local alerts from the nearest U.S. Embassy. You do not have to be a U.S. citizen to participate in this program.

More excellent travel information from the U.S. Department of State

https://travel.state.gov/content/travel/en/international-travel/before-you-go/travelers-checklist.html

Think Hazard is a great place to find simple international risk assessments.

https://www.thinkhazard.org/en/

Temple University has excellent information for international travelers.

https://finance.temple.edu/travel-planning/emergency-preparedness-abroad

American Red Cross Contacting Loved Ones

https://www.redcross.org/get-help/disaster-relief-and-recovery-services/contact-and-locate-loved-ones.html

Harvard Global Support Services Travel Tools and Resources

https://www.globalsupport.harvard.edu/travel

Notes

Day 27
Danger Will Robinson!

*The difference between being a victim and a survivor is often a low level of **situational** awareness.*

–Barry Eisler

Lost in Space was an iconic science fiction TV show that aired between 1965 and 1968 and has enjoyed a very healthy market in reruns through the years. This pioneering family, literally lost in space trying to find their way home, had a robot not very creatively named "Robot" that would warn the commander (Will Robinson) of ensuing danger by flailing his arms and having his lighted head pop up with a raised voice saying, "Danger Will Robinson, Danger!" Wouldn't that be great? One could walk around in life with something else evaluating your threats and hazards, and then immediately giving you feedback on impending dangers. Our ancestors used to do this for themselves. Militaries, law enforcement, and fire services are very good at it because their lives depend on it. It has only been within the last fifty years that we have completely walled ourselves off from sound, sight, and what used to be natural cues to act. Technology affords us many benefits; however, a downside to self-driving cars, things in our ears, and our faces on screens is lowered situational awareness. Situational awareness, or "SA," has many official definitions. Still, for simplicity, it is the ability to recognize and understand a situation or environment, and the capability to identify and assess any potential threats and take the necessary steps to address them. SA, like anything else, can be improved with practice and mindful intent. Having weather and traffic alerts on your phone will significantly enhance your local and macro situational awareness, as major events will be covered in the news, and you'll be notified officially on time. What about our personal space? This is where we need to improve and do better. When you are outside your home or driving, limit distractions. Music, games, and conversations are all great when we are stationary. When walking, driving, or spending time somewhere else, pay attention. Notice other people. Who is there and why? What are they up to? By simply paying attention, you are less of a target. Identify entry and exit points while walking and driving. You may have to leave a different way than you entered. Practice prediction. As you observe people, transportation modes, and mechanical infrastructure, assess whether your prediction of their next actions is accurate. Trust your intuition. If it looks or sounds bad or wrong, it probably is. Constantly assess your surroundings for threats. What could go wrong can go wrong. While knowledge is power and understanding the concepts above is crucial, there are practical steps you can take to regain the SA that the modern world has eroded. First, position yourself for observation. When you are out in public, always find a position that gives you the best observational advantage. Corners facing out are ideal. This keeps any possible threat in front of you, where you can see it. When you are standing in a crowded area, position yourself in front of a wall or other surface. This will help protect you by keeping people out of your blind spot. Eating at the back of the restaurant, facing the entrance, will give you the most observational advantage and more time for responding if necessary. Turning SA into a game can help motivate you to stay consistent. Have whoever is with you join in. Ask questions like these and see who can come up with the answer quickly: How many men/women are in the room? How many men have facial hair? How many children are there? How many people are wearing jackets? What color are people wearing the most? Doing this while boarding an aircraft is a great first run at who is with you. In addition to counting and observing, your ability to ascertain what is normal for a particular environment is important, too. Pay attention to what is going on around you at the places you go often. Are there usually a lot of people around? If so, what ages and genders? What is the noise level typically like? Marking what is normal will help alert you when something is out of the ordinary. When traveling to a new location, try to "mark" and gain a deeper understanding of your surroundings. If something seems "off" to you about someone or some place, pay attention. Intuition is a powerful thing. If you notice someone trying to blend in, stay aware of that as well. These are not sure signs of danger, but they can be. Macro and micro–SA are not difficult, but one must practice them to develop them well.

Your Turn: Learn to use your peripheral vision. Practice this while having your next conversation. Begin to observe what is happening in your peripheral vision while still listening and engaging. Additionally, learn to slow down and scan your environment. This comes naturally, but learn to be specific about what you are scanning for. Notice where exits are, barriers to avoid or use to your advantage, suspicious objects, or suspicious people. Next time you go somewhere, be purposeful about entering and exiting your location.

Pro Tip: Play Kim's game with your friends and family. The name is derived from Rudyard Kipling's 1901 novel *Kim*, in which the protagonist plays the game during his training as a spy. The game enhances a person's ability to observe and recall details and is utilized by youth groups and militaries worldwide. Collect several articles on a tray – knives, spoons, pencil, pen, stones, book, and so on – not more than about fifteen for the first few games, and cover the whole over with a cloth. Have others sit around, where they can see the tray, and uncover it for one minute. Then each participant must make a list on a piece of paper of all the articles they can remember. The one who remembers most wins the game. A simpler version could involve looking at all the items, then covering or taking away one, and secretly removing another object from it. Rather than being asked to list all the objects they saw on the tray, the tray is returned with one item missing, and the players are asked to identify that missing object.

Resources for Day 27: Danger Will Robinson!

There is a lot written and published on SA from military, law enforcement, and fire service sources, with hundreds of YouTube videos available. Two other great sources are below.

Maricopa County, Arizona Attorney's Office has a great discussion and measures for SA.

https://maricopacountyattorney.org/400/Situational-Awareness

Global Guardian discusses SA in the workplace.

https://www.globalguardian.com/global-digest/situational-awareness.

Notes

Day 28
Evacuation Decisions

Should I stay or should I go now? If I go, there will be trouble; if I stay, it will be double.

—The Clash from the Combat Rock Album 1982

At the beginning of this book, we discussed basic emergency preparedness, and when we prepared for certain specific hazards, we mentioned the term evacuation. But evacuation is not just leaving your current location and going somewhere else on your own. You may be part of a larger community effort that emergency planners have already taken into consideration. The larger your community, the more this is probably true. Find these plans from your town, city, or state planning officials. It is worth your time and effort to see what their initial ideas are in the face of a large-scale event. Large highways may be closed in various directions to create flow or counter-flow on roads that you need to know to leave. Some other concepts are useful in understanding evacuation planning. Horizontal evacuation can be thought of as increasing the distance from you and the hazard on the map. Vertical evacuation requires increases or decreases in elevation, typically combined with adding horizontal distance. High-rise buildings mostly require vertical evacuation; floods and particularly storm surges and tsunamis require sufficient vertical evacuation to escape inundation and runup. Large populations may need to use phased or staged evacuations. With enough notice, evacuations may be staggered by location, time/resources needed to evacuate, transportation capacity, or a combination. This is most used for tropical storms affecting densely populated areas. It may ease traffic loads and will give evacuees who need more time to evacuate a head start. Voluntary or recommended evacuation concentrates on people who are most vulnerable to a potential hazard and may need more time or additional resources to evacuate. Special traffic-control or transportation measures tend not to be implemented – or are done on a limited scale – for this type of evacuation. For mandatory evacuation, persons are "strongly urged" to relocate to a safer location. Personal discretion is not to be considered a deciding factor. A person who refuses to comply with a "mandatory" evacuation order may not be forcibly removed from his/her home; however, all public services will be suspended during a mandatory evacuation, and those failing to comply with a mandatory evacuation order may not be rescued or provided with other lifesaving assistance. If conditions continue to deteriorate, at some point, evacuation routes will be closed and emergency response curtailed. Intuitively, we may think to ourselves, "If I go in the opposite direction of the evacuation order, I'll get to where I want to faster, and there will be less congestion." Please do not do this! You could be evacuating directly into the danger that the evacuation order was meant to avoid. During an evacuation, time can be a critical and helpful factor, but only if you use it. Evacuate as early as possible when you feel you may need to do so. If the emergency wasn't that bad after evacuating, then you had a good drill! If you must evacuate, make sure every family member has their go-bag. Unplug all appliances before leaving. Turn off electricity, gas, and the main water valve. Of note is that you should not attempt to light the gas pilot upon return. Call the utility company. Tell someone outside of the emergency area where you are going, lock your home, and leave. To prepare for evacuation, avoid creating unnecessary tasks that consume valuable time. This behavior is called "milling" when one continues activities unnecessarily in the face of overwhelming fear and stress. Recognize it and fight it so you can properly evacuate.

Your Turn: For the relevant hazards and your individual situation, make evacuation plans. They may not all be the same. Then, combine your own common sense thinking with known official evacuation planning for your area. Are they the same? Come to some ground truth in your own mind about what you would do if you had to evacuate. Mark your evacuation plans on a paper map and keep them in your go-bag and car. You may not have access to a GPS or electronic maps when you evacuate.

Pro Tip: Using your own evacuation plans above, have an evacuation drill with your family using the routes you may need in an actual emergency. Make a mini vacation of it and go spend the night in a place you might evacuate to. This will build family resilience by helping you understand the plan, what is required, and what will happen when you get there. A real evacuation can be scary, so strive to make it a fun and positive activity. Be sure to include pets if you have them in this drill. Many make very poor evacuation decisions during real emergencies because they have not considered their pets.

Resources for Day 28: Evacuation Decisions

Understanding basic evacuation concepts and what your government may be planning can significantly aid your own evacuation planning. A great guide on this is below.

U.S. Federal Emergency Management Agency (FEMA) Planning Considerations: Evacuation and Shelter-in-Place

https://www.fema.gov/sites/default/files/2020-07/planning-considerations-evacuation-and-shelter-in-place.pdf

Notes

Day 29
During a Disaster

Strength does not come from physical capacity. It comes from an indomitable will.

–Mohandas Karamchand Gandhi

Emergency preparedness does not prevent disasters from happening. No one expects to be caught in a potentially dangerous and extreme situation such as a natural or human-caused disaster. If the unthinkable does occur, having the plans we have developed thus far and all the hazards thinking we have applied to the problems could make all the difference for you and your loved ones. If you are caught in a major emergency, follow the plans you have created thus far in this book. Get your go-bags ready to use or to evacuate in case of an emergency. Stay in a safe area or shelter if you have not been ordered to evacuate. In your home, a secure location may be a ground-floor interior room, closet, or bathroom. Be sure you have access to your go-bag and family communications plan in case you are in an emergency event that lasts for several days. Stay away from windows, skylights, and glass doors. Make sure you are safe before assisting others. Listen to your portable radio or television for important updates and instructions from local authorities. Remember to have a battery-powered radio in your go-bag. Some radios are now equipped with multiple power sources, such as batteries, solar panels, and a hand crank. If power is lost, see the concepts on Day 17.

Turn off major appliances and keep refrigerators and freezers closed. Use a generator with caution. Make sure conditions are safe before operating a portable generator. Only operate it outside away from windows, doors, or vents. Follow all manufacturers' instructions. Stay in your safe area and do not drive until the danger has passed. If you were ordered to evacuate, resist the temptation to return and check on your property before you are told to do so. As we mentioned during Day 28, learn how to shut off the gas valves, water, and electricity in your home and keep the tools handy for those purposes. Maintaining your previous preparations will be critically important during any emergency. It might take days to restore critical infrastructure and basic supplies. As with all disasters and emergencies, your level of preparedness will determine your quality of life in the weeks and months that follow. During the emergency, we need the skills from Days 21 and 22 more than ever to get us through this. Keep calm. Think. Make decisions with others based on the knowledge you have in the moment.

Your Turn: What would it be like to be in a disaster? Have these discussions now with your immediate family. See how they feel about things. What are their concerns? Work to address them in your planning. These discussions will build family resilience and further expose your family to planning and the resources available for such situations.

Pro Tip: There are plenty of disaster-related science shows and movies based on real-world events. Watch some now, being mindful of basic emergency preparedness concepts. Were the people in the shows prepared? How could they have done better?

Resources for Day 29: During a Disaster

U.S. Centers for Disease Control: Children and School Preparedness

https://www.cdc.gov/children-and-school-preparedness/before-during-after/index.html

California Governor's Office of Emergency Services

https://news.caloes.ca.gov/family-preparedness-are-you-ready-california/

ADT Home Safety Tips

https://www.adt.com/resources/home-safety-tips-for-natural-disasters

Food Safety Disaster Preparedness

https://www.foodsafety.gov/keep-food-safe/food-safety-in-disaster-or-emergency

Notes

Day 30
Disaster Recovery

Everyone deserves the chance to survive. I think of this every time I see another disaster. There are probably people dying who do not have to.

–James Hubbard

You have done a great job attending to everything in this book and have a substantial amount of knowledge, resources, and resiliency necessary to face the unexpected. You may have to use most of the other twenty-nine days of this book on Day 30. Now, hopefully, nobody in your family was hurt. When a disaster strikes, survivors face the painful task of rebuilding their lives. We should hesitate and not say "back to normal" because the future may not look like the past when communities are destroyed. So, what will we do now that it has happened? What would it be like if you lost your home and your job?

We must care for basic needs and keep businesses going while enduring stress and trauma. This is the true essence of community resilience. Many communities disappear and businesses dissolve after a disaster. On top of this, we must manage multiple bureaucratic processes with competing guidance, which is a confusing and frustrating journey at a moment when people expect the government to show up and help. Getting our families, neighbors, and communities to some basic level of functionality is an overall priority. First things first. When we know the disaster has come to an end, we must take care of ourselves physically, emotionally, and spiritually. This may be a long process that could take days, weeks, and even months.

We also need to assess the damage to homes, businesses, and community infrastructure. You will not be alone, as your entire community, government, and numerous non-profit organizations will come together to support you. There may be various forms of assistance and shelter available. Be sure to look for and ask about food, cleaning materials, and other forms of assistance. You may be surprised by how much will be available temporarily to help you through. Before we can move back in, we may have to give our homes some first aid, either structurally or by drying them out. Although it's not our direct responsibility, the community will need to restore utilities, which may result in a power outage. We may need to clean up not only our property's mess, but also the entire community's, which may require extensive debris removal and special sanitation priorities, such as road clearing. Check your home for cracks and damage, including the roof, chimneys, and foundation. Be careful when returning to a property. File an insurance claim as soon as you are able and inform local authorities about health and safety concerns.

Take pictures of the damage to both the house and its contents for insurance claims. Remember, when electricity is lost for several hours or days, frozen and refrigerated food may not be safe to eat. Do not refreeze thawed food. Throw away all food that has been under flood waters, except canned food, but wash and sanitize the cans before opening. All food that cannot be saved should be double-bagged for normal trash disposal or buried at least two feet deep. Be sure to check for water safety issues or if there is a boil water order in effect. In warm weather, empty water out of birdbaths, tires, flowerpots, and other containers to limit mosquito larvae growth.

Your Turn: Imagine a tornado or flood destroying your entire community. What would happen next? You can find out by going to your local authority's disaster recovery plan. Most towns, cities, counties, and states have them on public- facing websites in the Office of Emergency Management (there are many variations of the naming conventions where these might be held). If you are unable to find it, call and ask at the town or city manager's office. Fire and police departments are helpful sources of information, too, about disaster response and recovery plans.

Pro Tip: The better prepared you are, the faster you will be able to recover from a disaster. Is your family able to sleep outside in a tent on your property? Do you have multiple ways of purifying and storing water? Cooperation is key. How can you and your neighbors plan for disaster recovery on your street or in your neighborhood?

Resources for Day 30: Disaster Recovery

U.S. Federal Emergency Management Agency (FEMA) Disaster Recovery

https://www.ready.gov/recovering-disaster

American Psychological Association: Recovering Emotionally from Disasters

https://www.apa.org/topics/disasters-response/recovering

American Red Cross Emotional Recovery After a Disaster

https://www.redcross.org/get-help/disaster-relief-and-recovery-services/recovering-emotionally.html

American Red Cross Disaster Relief and Recovery Services

https://www.redcross.org/get-help/disaster-relief-and-recovery-services.html

U.S. Government Disaster Assistance

https://www.disasterassistance.gov/

U.S. Small Business Administration (SBA) Recover from Disasters

https://www.usa.gov/disasters-and-emergencies

Notes

Day 31
Your Know Bag and
Community Building

What can man achieve through virtuous striving that is more important than knowledge?

—Erasmus

Congratulations! You've come to the end of the book. I wrote this book for most people in most situations. If you have at least started on the tasks and concepts for all thirty previous days, then you are better prepared than 90% of the rest of the planet for emergencies and disasters. And while this is the end of the book, it is only the start of a lifelong preparedness journey. Rather than the end, it is only the beginning. Schedule time on your calendar at least once a month to revisit days that may need adjustments or improvements. If you move somewhere, you'll need to review everything and adjust. If your family situation changes in terms of the number of people in your household, you will need to adjust that, too. There are many disasters we have not focused on, such as tsunamis and terrorist attacks. If you are concerned about these and many others, then do your research and add to your planning. You got this. You now know all the basic principles, and just like other preparedness kits you have built, this book has helped you create your "know bag" to take with you wherever you go. At the end of this chapter, I have included my favorite apps, websites, and books to keep you interested and involved in your own personal and professional emergency preparedness. As I mentioned in the introduction, emergency preparation is something many people plan to do tomorrow, but tomorrow never comes. It is the icing on life's cake. Something that makes it better and sweeter later. By doing one thing a day for thirty-one days, your mindset for preparing for disasters has changed. You now know that emergency preparedness is the flour of life's cake, or rather an indispensable component. You were not too busy to put it off, and you stopped making excuses.

Through all of this, you have significantly increased your resilience. Now that you have vastly improved the emergency preparedness of yourself and everyone around you, it is time to dive deeper to create an authentic culture of preparedness in our communities. First, consider volunteering and donating. During disaster response, affected communities depend heavily on local and national volunteer organizations to provide trained volunteers and much-needed donated supplies. Get involved today by donating to or volunteering with a reputable organization. When emergencies are not happening, we can also be involved with training and educating the community. As you have already seen, you could help save countless lives by taking simple actions to prepare your community or organization before a disaster strikes. There are numerous free training courses and educational tools available to help you and others prepare for, respond to, and recover from disasters or emergencies.

Despite what some may think or have seen in informational campaigns or previous training, messages of emergency preparedness are messages of hope and love, not doom and gloom. I care enough about you to write this book. You love your family and those around you, and they love you. Involve them and your community in emergency and disaster preparedness so we can all live happier, healthier lives. And if something goes wrong, we've got this!

Resources for Day 31: Your Know Bag and Community Building

National Volunteer Organizations Active in Disaster is a safe and reputable way to find organizations in your area and make donations.

https://www.nvoad.org/donate/

While there are hundreds of organizations in the United States and around the world organizing volunteer efforts, major ones in the United States include the American Red Cross, Salvation Army, Samaritan's Purse, and Team Rubicon.

American Red Cross

https://www.redcross.org/volunteer/volunteer-opportunities/disaster-volunteer.html

Salvation Army

https://salarmveds.org/

Samaritan's Purse

https://www.samaritanspurse.org/

Team Rubicon

https://rollcall-events.teamrubiconusa.org/

Help train in your community by seeing what is out there for you that you might be interested in. Locally focused opportunities might exist in your area under the names of Community Emergency Response Team (CERT), Medical. Reserve Corps (MRC), and t h e National Weather Service Weather-Ready Nation Ambassador Program.

National CERT Association

https://nationalcert.org/

U.S. Federal Emergency Management Agency (FEMA) CERT Information

https://www.fema.gov/emergency-managers/individuals-communities/preparedness-activities-webinars/community-emergency-response-team

Medical Reserve Corps

https://aspr.hhs.gov/MRC/Pages/index.aspx

National Weather Service Weather-Ready Nation Ambassador Program

https://www.weather.gov/wrn/ambassadors

There are dozens of ways to continue to learn and grow in this area. Consider searching for courses with search cues like disaster, crisis, and emergency in open courses and open university settings, such as Coursera, Future Learn, Harvard Online, and many others. Most are free.

The U.S. National Disaster and Emergency Management University, through its online portal, also known as the Emergency Management Institute, offers hundreds of courses for free. You'll have to register first, and most of these courses are for professionals working in emergency management or public safety, but many are for individual emergency preparedness.

https://training.fema.gov/is/

Notes

_____

_____

_____

_____

_____

_____

_____

_____

_____

Top 10 Emergency Preparedness Mobile Apps

Having emergency preparedness apps on your phone ensures you receive real-time alerts, warnings, and vital updates during a crisis. These apps provide quick access to safety tips, shelter locations, communication tools, and first aid guidance. They help you make informed decisions faster, even when traditional communication systems are down. They also enhance personal safety and improve your ability to respond effectively in emergencies.

1. **FEMA Mobile App:** Real-time weather and emergency alerts, shelter finder, planning checklists, disaster assistance info.

2. **American Red Cross Emergency App** customizable weather alerts, shelter maps, step-by-step hazard guidance.

3. **American Red Cross First Aid App** offline medical instructions, quizzes, bilingual support.

4. **American Red Cross Pet First Aid App** offers offline medical instructions for a variety of pets, quizzes, and bilingual support.

5. **PulsePoint Respond** connects with local 911 dispatch to notify nearby CPR-trained bystanders of cardiac emergencies.

6. **Earthquake Network** crowdsourced global earthquake early-warning app using smartphone sensors; issues alerts and shares shake data.

7. **Wildfire Info / Cal Fire Ready for Wildfire App** real-time wildfire maps and alerts—especially useful in high-risk areas.

8. **Disaster Alert** global multi-hazard alerts, including natural and technological events; consolidates multiple warning sources.

9. **Air Force Ready is** not just for members of the United States Air Force. A great source for planning and all-hazard info.

10. **Psychological First Aid** for disaster mental health with quick guides for individuals and those they are helping to cope with emergencies and disasters. Step-by-step processes for rendering assistance.

Top 10 Emergency Preparedness Websites

Researching and understanding emergency preparedness websites helps you access reliable, up-to-date information from trusted sources like FEMA, the CDC, and NOAA. These sites offer tools, checklists, and guidance tailored to various hazards and community needs. Staying informed empowers you to make better emergency preparedness decisions and build resilience. It also ensures your plans and actions align with national standards and best practices.

1. Ready Gov www.Ready.gov

   The official FEMA site for individual, family, and community preparedness. Offers planning tools, checklists, and hazard-specific guidance.

2. Federal Emergency Management Agency www.FEMA.gov

   Comprehensive U.S. federal emergency management site offering disaster response updates, grants, recovery info, and planning resources.

3. Center for Disease Control Emergency Preparedness and Response www.cdc.gov/emergency/index.html

   Provides public health guidance, emergency alerts, and preparedness resources for pandemics, natural disasters, and bioterrorism.

4. American Red Cross www.redcross.org

   Offers emergency apps, first aid advice, and preparedness

checklists tailored for families, schools, and workplaces.

5. National Weather Service www.weather.gov

    Provides timely forecasts, alerts, and safety tips for extreme weather events, including hurricanes, tornadoes, and blizzards.

6. Department of Homeland Security www.DHS.gov

    Covers national security topics, critical infrastructure protection, and coordination across emergency disciplines.

7. Disaster Assistance www.DisasterAssistance.gov

    Central portal to apply for federal disaster assistance, locate shelters, and access recovery resources.

8. U.S. Fire Administration www.usfa.gov

    Part of FEMA, this site promotes fire safety, prevention programs, and community risk reduction strategies.

9. Health Emergency Preparedness Information Gateway (ASPR TRACIE) www.asprtracie.hhs.gov

    A health emergency preparedness site from the Department of Health and Human Services, offering technical resources, planning tools, and best practices for healthcare systems.

10. National Hurricane Center www.nhc.noaa.gov

    Specialized NOAA site with hurricane tracking, preparedness tips, and real-time advisories.

Top 10 Emergency Preparedness Books

It is hard to just pick ten! This list features ten highly regarded books on emergency preparedness, suitable for professionals, students, and individuals seeking to enhance their knowledge and readiness. Hopefully, over time, you will develop your own list based on your needs and make recommendations to others.

1. *When All Hell Breaks Loose: Stuff You Need to Survive When Disaster Strikes* by Cody Lundin. (Gibbs Smith, 2007)

2. *The Unthinkable: Who Survives When Disaster Strikes—and Why* by Amanda Ripley. (Second Edition, 2024)

3. *Handbook of Emergency Management Concepts: A Step-by-Step Approach* by Michael L. Madigan. (CRC Press, 2009)

4. *Disaster Operations and Decision Making* by Roger C. Huder. (Wiley, 2013)

5. *Emergency Management: The American Experience 1900–2010 edited* by Claire B. Rubin. (Routledge, 2012)

6. *102 Minutes* by Jim Dwyer and Kevin Flynn (Times Books, 2011)

7. *The Disaster Recovery Handbook: A Step-by-Step Plan to*

Ensure Business Continuity and Protect Vital Operations, Facilities, and Assets by Michael Wallace and Lawrence Webber. (AMACOM, 2017)

8. *You're It* by Leonard Marcus, Eric McNutty, Joseph Henderson, and Barry Dorn (Hachette Book Group, 2019)

9. *The Big Ones* by Dr. Lucy Jones (Doubleday, 2018)

10. *The Gift of Fear* by Gavin de Becker. (Dell Publishing, 1997)

Annual Emergency Preparedness Calendar

Planning and using a calendar help ensure that important tasks and deadlines are not forgotten, increasing efficiency and reducing stress. It allows individuals and organizations to allocate time and resources effectively, prioritize responsibilities, and stay on track toward goals. Calendaring emergency preparedness activities ensures timely training and drills for you and your family, while also allowing for community engagement. Overall, it promotes accountability, readiness, and proactive decision-making. The dates below are for the United States; many other countries have essential planning activities as well.

January

<u>National Radon Action Month</u> (Environmental Protection Agency): Encourages home radon testing and mitigation to reduce health risks.

February

<u>Earthquake Awareness Month</u> (varied by state): Promotes awareness and preparedness activities, especially in earthquake-prone areas.

March

<u>Flood Safety Awareness Week</u> (National Oceanic and Atmospheric Administration/National Weather Service): Promotes flood risk awareness and encourages insurance and

evacuation planning.

American Red Cross Month: Recognizes the contributions of the Red Cross in disaster response and preparedness.

April

National Tsunami Awareness Week (National Oceanic and Atmospheric Administration): Promotes coastal safety and tsunami evacuation planning.

National Public Health Week (American Public Health Association/Centers for Disease Control): Focuses on health resilience during disasters.

National Volunteer Week: Celebrates the role of volunteers in emergency response and recovery.

May

National Wildfire Awareness Month (U.S. Forest Service/Federal Emergency Management Agency): Encourages defensible space creation andwildfire evacuation planning.

National Hurricane Preparedness Week (National Oceanic and Atmospheric Administration/Federal Emergency Management Agency): Promotes storm readiness, family plans, and emergency kits.

Building Safety Month (International Code Council/Federal Emergency Management Agency): Highlights safe building practices to reduce disaster vulnerability.

June

Start of Hurricane Season – June 1 (National Oceanic and Atmospheric Administration): Atlantic hurricane season starts;

readiness campaigns launch a little prior to generally.

National Pet Preparedness Month (Federal Emergency Management Agency): Encourages planning for pets in all emergency plans.

July

Extreme Heat Safety Awareness (Centers for Disease Control/National Oceanic and Atmospheric Administration): Highlights the dangers of heat illness and the importance of cooling centers and hydration.

August

Back to School Preparedness (Ready.gov/Federal Emergency Management Agency): Promotesfamily emergency planning, communication, and school safety.

September

National Preparedness Month (Ready.gov Federal Emergency Management Agency): Major preparedness campaign focusing on risk identification, planning, kits, and community actions.

October

Fire Prevention Week (National Fire Protection Association/Federal Emergency Management Agency): Focuses on home fire safety and escape plans.

Great Shake Out Earthquake Drill – 3rd Thursday: Nationwide earthquake drill promoting Drop, Cover, and Hold On.

Cybersecurity Awareness Month (Critical Infrastructure Security Agency/Department of Homeland Security):

Emphasizes cyber hygiene and continuity of digital operations.

November

<u>Winter Weather Awareness</u> (National Oceanic and Atmospheric Administration/National Weather Service): Focuses on cold weather hazards, heating safety, and vehicle preparedness.

December

<u>National Impaired Driving Prevention Month</u> (National Highway Traffic Safety Administration): Promotes public safety and emergency response awareness during holiday travel.

www.ingramcontent.com/pod-product-compliance
Lightning Source LLC
Chambersburg PA
CBHW071728120626
46550CB00002B/428